THE JOY OF COLD REVENGE

Kam Kavanaugh

PALADIN PRESS
BOULDER, COLORADO

The Joy of Cold Revenge
by Kam Kavanaugh
Copyright © 1986 by Kam Kavanaugh

ISBN 0-87364-385-2
Printed in the United States of America

Published by Paladin Press, a division of
Paladin Enterprises, Inc., P.O. Box 1307,
Boulder, Colorado 80306, USA.
(303) 443-7250

Direct inquiries and/or orders to the above address.

Neither the author nor the publisher assumes
any responsibility for the use or misuse of
information contained in this book. This book
is presented for entertainment purposes only.

Contents

To Sandy Jones of Immonen Road

Introduction

There comes a time in all of our lives when we've had enough. A time when we feel we can take no more. A time when we've been dumped on one time too many. Every day we read and hear stories about people who have been screwed over by bullies and those petty little Nazi-type officials. We hear about people who have been driven around the bend and forced to take some drastic action. Some action that forced them into the role of breaking the law. Had there been justice in the first place, there would have been no need for drastic action. There would have been no need for a good, hard-working citizen finding himself charged with a crime. And don't think for one minute that the courts give consideration to the mitigating circumstances that forced the law-abiding citizen into an act of crime. The courts will never take a position that their actions, or their failure to act, were a contributing factor to a criminal act. When these things happen, we always hear the cry of the self-righteous, "There ought to be a law." What law? What justice?

It doesn't take a person with anything between the ears too long to come to the conclusion that our system of justice does not provide justice to the ordinary citizen in this country. The average person without connections doesn't have a chance of receiving justice in our legal system. Our courts, with their corrupted judges, their greedy lawyers, their petty administrators, and their politically ambitious prosecutors, have all but done away with the Bill of Rights. This ambitious, greedy scum of our society has destroyed the meaning of The Con-

1

stitution. They have twisted and used it to their own gain at the cost of the rights of the individuals for whom it was meant to protect. At best, we're left with a Bill of Wrongs. Wrongs perpetrated on the American public by the greedy scum and parasites of our society.

What then can the honest, hard-working citizen do? How can those of us who have been dumped on and wronged get some measure of justice? Sue the bastard! That's the biggest joke of all.

It is usually very difficult to tell just exactly who your lawyer is working for. Before hiring an attorney, bear in mind that he is looking out for his own best interest—his bank account. And you can be certain that no lawyer will do anything to upset the stratified sycophantic association he has with the judges.

No lawyer who is financially ambitious will work too hard for his client if he sees the judge is in sympathy with the opposition. Long after you are gone, he will have to appear before that judge on other cases. Remember, the most prejudiced person in the courtroom, other than the parties to the action, is the judge. These corrupted judges can make a suit go either way simply in the way they rule on objections. Add to this the power they have in their rulings on motions, and one finds they are the ones who orchestrate the outcome of any given case. The lawyer who has fallen out of favor with a judge will very likely never win a future case before that judge. In our present corrupted justice system, it is necessary for the lawyers to be sycophantic to the judges, who in turn look out for the interest of the common parasites of our society. One thing is certain, the hard-working citizens of this country cannot expect justice from our courts. Nor can they expect a semblance or even a trace of justice through local, state, or federal government agencies. They can strike out in anger, but what will that achieve? Beyond a small measure of immediate satisfaction, nothing of lasting value.

Take for example the police with their gestapo mentality who will bring charges of assault and menacing, making the victim of a wrongdoing the official villain. Acting on impulse has proven to be the wrong thing to do when finding yourself ripped off or dumped on by the parasites of our society. Impulse actions are largely regarded as anti-social by the scum who administer the justice system. Should one strike out in such violence as to seriously injure or kill a tormentor, he will be charged accordingly and the price is too much to pay for eliminating a single piece of scum from our society.

So there you are, alone with nowhere to turn. Your thoughts turn toward ways of getting even. But why just get even? Why only an eye for an eye, a tooth for a tooth? That only puts you back to square one, and you still stand a good chance of having the gestapo on your back. The answer is revenge, and revenge is always best when it is cold. Cold revenge is the ultimate tool with which to get even.

Just what is *cold revenge?* It is the revenge achieved long after the heat of passion has cooled. Cold revenge is when you take your satisfaction long after your enemy has concluded he is home free. Cold revenge is when you come like a ghost from the past and smash your enemy like a bug—the one who dumped on you and thought he got away with it. Cold revenge is more than getting even. It is exacting a debt and its interest. Cold revenge is winning in the largest sense of the word. It wins so completely that there is no comeback—you have already done it all.

Unlike striking out in the heat of passion, cold revenge requires patience and planning so that revenge is effective and causes maximum damage. You may think that killing your enemy would inflict maximum damage. Would it really? Killing your enemy would actually put him out of his misery. Do you want to do that? Of course not. You want to increase his misery. How about blowing off his kneecap? If your enemy deserves it, yes. But such acts of violence are rarely necessary to satisfy your appetite for revenge.

If your revenge truly runs deep, such as avenging a long-standing feud that pushed you to the wall or the rape of your preteenaged daughter whose attacker walked freely away from court, then this book is *not* for you. There are only a few things you can do to enemies like that. A study of the techniques used in the Middle East will prove most helpful.

However, for those who want the garden variety of cold

revenge, this book provides a series of useful and effective methods of adding misery to the scum that dumped on you. One thing to remember is that effective cold revenge must come like a ghost from the past. And this must be planned—if the hand is tipped too soon, your action could be ineffectual.

The techniques outlined in this book have all been used successfully. This does not mean there are no risks involved, and it is not implied that any of these acts are legal. These days, most actions that upset someone else could be considered a crime. Bear this in mind and act accordingly. Certainly don't brag about your accomplishment. If the purpose of your cold revenge is to have something to brag to others about, then you should examine your motives more closely.

Recently there have been several "get even" books on the market. All of these books hedge the issue. They use such terms as *mark, victim, harassment,* and *trick* along with a host of other soft terms. In order to make a real impression, you must think in hard terms such as *enemy* and *cold revenge.* Anything less is merely playing games.

1.
Ethics of Cold Revenge

The perpetual question, "Does the end justify the means?" is meaningless when applied to cold revenge. There are only two sets of questions to answer. First, does your enemy deserve what you have planned? Did your enemy do things that adversely affected your life? Did your enemy do something that left you with a poorer quality of life? Did your enemy do something that unjustly enriched himself at the cost of something of value to you? If you can honestly answer one or more of these questions affirmatively, then you are well within your moral rights in doing what you plan. You have every right to seek the revenge you deserve. And in doing so, you place yourself at the vanguard of those few who say they have had enough. You have placed yourself among the elite who take charge of their lives, and refuse to allow the scum of our society to climb another rung on their ladder at the cost of others' freedom. You will be able to look back on your life and tell your posterity that you did something about the wrongs of the world, and did not grovel for your existence.

The second set of questions you may want to consider are: Did your enemy exercise any ethics when he dumped on you? Was he considerate? Did he think of your rights and feelings? Has your enemy shown any signs of remorse for his act of dumping on you? If the answer is no, then you need not consider fair play, and you can rest assured that you are doing the right thing. Your enemy has clearly demonstrated that he is motivated by self-interest at the cost of others. He has shown that he would perform a similar act in the future if it meets his needs and desire. Your enemy has placed himself among the slugs and parasites of our society. He has lost any respect or rights of consideration one is usually afforded in society. He has declared himself to be your enemy.

Should you have second thoughts about your acts of cold revenge, you must decide if these feelings are the result of the fear of being caught, or the feelings of years of brainwashing to turn the other cheek. One of the reasons the scum of our society have gotten away with pushing people around for so long is that ridiculous attitude of turning the other cheek. Other societies have been known to turn the other cheek and all it got them was mass extermination. Being meek will only get you more abuse. You let a piece of scum walk on you once and you have given carte blanche for all the other parasites to take a shot at you. You can become a professional victim to these scum bags. You and you alone must decide where that line is beyond which you will retreat no more. You must decide the time for an all-out effort aimed at cold revenge. Turning the other cheek will only get that bashed in, too. One last thought on turning the other cheek: the world does not care for the abused. The world cheers for those who fight back.

The consequence of being caught depends greatly on the act you plan. Most attacks of revenge would not result in a felony charge. If your act of revenge, however, is a felony, then perhaps you should rethink the problem and consider an action less serious. An act does not have to be a felony to be effective, and, in fact, if it is, you may create sympathy for your enemy. This would of course be counterproductive. Remember, acts against institutions such as banks, government agencies, and large corporations are often treated as felonious regardless of their magnitude. If you are obsessed with getting caught, you probably will, and this book really isn't for you. Read it for entertainment and leave the joy of cold revenge to those with more determination. For those who have that burning desire to right a wrong, it is highly recommended that rather than worrying about getting caught, you plan your tactics to include safeguards against capture.

There are a few ethical issues in revenge techniques that should be kept in mind. The first is that one's concern with the ethics of cold revenge varies inversely to one's personal interest in the issue. When we are not directly concerned, when we are not the dumpee, our morality overflows. That is why the courts look poorly on the acts of cold revenge. And the courts will particularly frown on them if they should be against a member of their tight-knit group. This ties in with the second issue, which is that judging the ethics of cold revenge is dependent upon the relative position of those who sit in judgment. Your enemy will not look favorably on your acts and those who are neutral will cheer you on as long as you are winning. Should something go wrong, they will all line up on the side of the enemy. Remember, these are the self-righteous people who always say there ought to be a law. These are the people who are neither here nor there. They are the sunshine patriots, your fair weather friends. They would never plant a tree under which they would not sit; they would never help put a star on the flag.

The third ethical issue of cold revenge is that any effective act on your part against your enemy will automatically be judged by him as unethical, because he cannot see where he has done wrong. However, the same act against you could be considered as good sport.

Fundamentally, the ethics of cold revenge are simply that you must do what you think is right. Many people will tell you that if you've been wronged, take it to court. Anyone who hasn't fallen off the turnip wagon yesterday can tell you, that is a joke. Since you can't expect justice from the courts or the authorities, it is no longer a point of ethics. Going outside the courts cannot be considered unethical when the courts themselves reek of corruption. You have to do it yourself if anything is to be done at all. The bullies must be shown that they can't hide behind their friends in the political and justice systems. The sooner more people revenge on those who dump on them, the sooner this country will get back to being run by ordinary citizens. These are the people who work, pay their taxes; those who deserve a fair shake in the system, which was originally conceived with them in mind but which has strayed into the hands of bullies, corrupted gestapo agents, unjust courts, and ambitious officials.

2.
Selecting Your Enemy

The term *enemy* is used in this book rather than words such as *target, mark,* or *victim,* because when you set out to get cold revenge, you must think of it as a war tactic. To think in terms of *target, mark,* or *victim* will create sympathy, which leads to mistakes. If this happens, see how much sympathy your enemy has for you. Your enemy will most likely be one of those detestable people who takes a lot and gives little. He certainly deserves the title *enemy* and the revenge treatment that goes with it.

Who are your enemies? If you have a long list, then maybe you should rethink the word *enemy.* If you seek revenge against many people you know, then perhaps the revenge you seek is really against yourself. There are many bitter people in this world who believe the world owes them a debt, and anything that goes wrong has to be someone else's fault. These people often orchestrate their own downfall. They are not necessarily stupid or poorly educated; in fact, many are college graduates. The joy of cold revenge is not for this type of person. To give them a taste of revenge would be like offering a drink to an alcoholic: they could never get enough. Actually, they are no better than those who deserve a measure of cold revenge. If you see yourself in this picture, you should get some books on self-analysis and shelve this book for the time being. You cannot spend your entire life seeking revenge.

Enemies, properly speaking, should be few and deserving. An enemy should be a person that no one would miss if they simply disappeared from the face of this planet. Your enemy should not simply be someone who has annoyed you. Everyone is annoyed by someone at one time or another. Your enemy is a person whom many others feel the same way about. If you find you have an enemy that others think of as a decent person, then you should look at yourself and evaluate if you are the problem. Rarely will a deserving bastard be thought of as anything but just that by the vast majority of people. The parasites of society can fool a few people for a short time, but not for long. Therefore, make sure your enemy truly deserves the cold revenge you plan to bestow on him.

A profile of the people who are usually on someone's revenge list shows them as petty, small-minded people who push others around for their own self-esteem. The Nazis drew on this class of people to obtain manpower for the gestapo and to staff the concentration camps. It is from these people that our police and petty civil servants are recruited. It then follows that anything you do to annoy our police or civil servants is deserving. It also follows that anything you do won't be looked on lightly by the police or courts, because they are of the same mold.

Why, you might ask, are these parasites in control of our society? Why, indeed? This is a question that is often asked, and one which can be debated on different levels. The best answer is simple and obvious. In a stagnant society, as in a swamp, the scum surfaces. Our society has been stagnant for too many years. People are affluent enough to let the petty rip-off artist have his fun. We have allowed these things to go on for so long that the scum has become a solid crust over our society. We have laughed at those who protested the invasion of these parasites. We have been so full of brotherly love that we allowed the scum to take control of society. It is time that we took back what is ours—control of our lives. A good place to begin is with a dose of cold revenge against those who have been dumping on people for years and getting away with it. This is a place where you can stand up and be counted. A place where you can show that you too have some of the courage our forefathers had in making this country. It is certain that they did not intend this land to be run by the scum now in control. This action must be taken now, or there will be a much larger problem in the future that can perhaps only be solved by anarchy.

Assuming that you determine your enemy deserves what you intend for him, you can now go forward with your plans for cold revenge. Don't get impatient, don't go off half-cocked, and don't jump the gun. This is one case where time is on your side. Unless your enemy is terminally ill, you have plenty of time, and since time is on your side, you should make good use of it. One thing that will help to keep you from getting impatient is remembering that revenge is the only dish that tastes sweetest when served cold.

Let's look at some of the common parasites of our society who might well deserve an ample serving of cold revenge. There is, of course, the ever-present landlord or apartment manager. This parasite almost always appears on a cold revenge list of the young, or those who are forced to dwell in the rental properties. He is usually from the same mold as gestapo agents, and has personality traits common with the Nazis. He also possesses a tendency toward greed as do all petty parasites of any society. Not all managers and owners are bad, but the good ones don't stay in the business for long. A good rule of thumb is that you either have a bad manager or you will soon have one.

The way landlords usually screw the tenant is on deposits. Cleaning deposits are seldom returned by these parasites, even if you spend days cleaning the unit and leave it in better condition than when you moved in. Some managers also have ways to harass tenants to force them to move out earlier than the prescribed time, thus tenants lose all or part of their deposit. Some managers claim damage to the unit and go to court with a claim, which is granted without your even knowing. To add insult to injury, your wage gets garnished. This type of action certainly calls for cold revenge not only on the manager but also on the judge.

Among some of the most deserving of cold revenge are institutions such as banks and insurance companies. These are followed closely by lawyers, judges, doctors, dentists, stock brokers, and real estate agents who are often apartment managers. Anyone who has had a brush with the law will undoubtedly find that police officers, sheriff deputies, judges, court personnel, along with newspaper and television reporters, all have the gestapo mentality.

Public utility companies such as telephone, gas, and electricity have all managed to get themselves high on the list of deserving a measure of cold revenge. It is amazing to see how these quasi-government organizations take their position so seriously that they think they hold the power of life and death over their customers. We've all heard of cases where these petty bullies have cut off service, which resulted in someone's death. Need more be said?

Then there is the garage mechanic who charged you for work he didn't do. And what about the judge in small claims court who ruled in the mechanic's favor, and later you found out the judge gets free service from that garage? Don't for one minute think this doesn't happen throughout this country. Our judges serve as collection agents and are rewarded well for their part in this massive fraud called courts of law.

Another parasite that has been sucking the blood of society for many years and has gained a good rubber-stamp working relationship with the corrupted judges are the employment agencies that victimize the young secretaries. They are in collusion with the employers who split the employment fees. The girls are usually not employed long enough to pay the fee and end up in small claims court. The employer who uses these agencies keeps a steady stream of girls going through the office for a percentage of the placement fee.

There are collection agencies that use the courts as collectors by having the judge order payment of a bill that has been turned over for collection. If the bill isn't paid, it is contempt of court that can and often does result in a jail sentence. This, in effect, is a debtor's prison. In these cases both the collection agency and the judge certainly deserve anything that happens to them. There is no doubt that cold revenge is too good for this class of scum in our society.

Yes, these are typical cases that surely deserve a measure of cold revenge. There are lots of other jerks that also should be smashed like bugs for the crap they pull on society. The typewriter repairman who charges you more than the machine is worth for fixing it, and it only lasted ten days over the thirty-day warranty. The hardware store that sells you a defective water heater and tells you that your only recourse is the manufacturer over a thousand miles away. And the printer who promised your letterhead in three weeks and still doesn't have it three months later. And if you cancel, this piece of scum goes to small claims court where his good friend is the judge. This list goes on and on. There are no limits to the ways of being screwed over in our corrupt society. All you can do is protect yourself as well as you can and hope for the best. If you do get shafted, it won't do you any good to go to the Better Business Bureau, the local prosecutor, the police, the state Consumer Protection Agency, or any other agency. In fact, you are better off not to make any noise at all if you plan on a course of cold revenge. Remember, the law is on the side of the corrupted and in going to the law, you will be putting yourself on the suspect list should something deserving happen to the parasite. So, to make cold revenge work, you must learn to keep your own counsel. Don't complain and don't explain.

After the passion and outrage have passed and you have had time to think it over, then decide if the wrongdoer is worth smashing like a bug. Is it worth your time and what it will cost you? Do you have other things that are more important to do than waste time on the scum bag in question? If so, forget it. If your heart and head aren't in it, you'll only make a mess of it and land yourself in trouble.

But if you still feel you've been dumped on, then you have an enemy. You have a cause, indeed, a worthy cause, and the world welcomes you to the class of those who are strong enough to stand up and be counted.

3.
Organizing the Operation

If you have determined that your enemy is deserving of a measure of cold revenge, and if you have no reservations about what you are about to do, your next step is to organize your operation.

The first thing to do is collect information about your enemy and his associates. Never overlook your enemy's associates who may be your enemy's only strength. Your enemy's strengths are just as important as his weaknesses and neither should be overlooked. If your enemy is an individual, rather than an institution, corporation, or government agency, your information will be considerably different. In any event, anything you learn about your enemy can prove useful and do not overlook small details. If your enemy is an institution, corporation, or government agency, you should seriously consider that they will have many resources to counterattack your revenge. Your actions will have to be serious to phase out these organizations. And you can be sure there will be an investigation. Is this what you want? It may be far better to determine the individual responsible for dumping on you and make that individual your enemy.

Unless you have something very specific in mind, it is suggested that you leave the exact method of revenge undecided until you have gathered all information on your enemy. Often, methods of revenge will come to light after information gathering that would have never been thought of before. However, the main reason for waiting to decide the method is to discover weaknesses in your enemy. Everyone has an Achilles' heel

15

somewhere. Something that you had not thought of at the beginning of the operation often comes to light that will be far more damaging to your enemy than anything else ever could. You can hit your enemy in a psychological soft spot.

Among those individuals who are most deserving of cold revenge, we often find a mortal weakness regarding sex. The bullies of the world pride themselves on their sexuality. However, it is often perverted, and this can be a powerful tool against them. With these bullies, this perverted trait is often pederasty. Discovering and exposing this trait will be all the cold revenge you need.

There is no limit to the information you can collect about an individual. You can learn everything down to his shoe size, license plate number, social security number, street address, post office box number, and the route he uses to go to and from work. Does he have a mistress on the side? Perhaps discovering something like this will be all you need to get your revenge. All you have to do is blow his cover. But when you do that, make sure the timing is right. That way you'll do a really good job of it.

By the time you have gathered all the necessary information about your enemy, you will have decided what action to take. Actually, you will probably have more than one choice in your plan of action. It is suggested that you plan an alternate course of action in case your primary one is unworkable or impractical. The alternate plan requires the same detailed thought as the primary plan.

Now, also, is the time to start gathering the necessary supplies for the operation. These supplies must be obtained well in advance of the actual operation. They must be obtained far from your home and far from the location of the attack. If an item must be purchased always use cash in small bills. Buy when the store is busy and do not draw attention to yourself. Should you need several items to effect your plan or make an assembly, buy each item in a separate place. Never allow any item to be traced back to you. This point cannot be emphasized enough.

At this stage of involvement, you may find yourself caught up in the excitement of the chase. You may become so excited that you want to share it with someone. Don't do it—never let anyone know what you are doing. If two people know a secret, it is no longer a secret. Even best friends have been known to sell out. Recall those lines in the book *1984* by George Orwell: *"Under the spreading chestnut tree, I sold you and you sold me."* Many a girlfriend has turned in her boyfriend for something she didn't quite approve of. And very often she disapproves of everything should the couple split up. Remember, wives turn in their husbands, especially when they become ex-husbands. Of course, these betrayals go both ways, so work alone.

This is probably a good place to say that the masculine pronouns he, his, and him are used in this book but refer to both sexes. Women, too, seek cold revenge. This book is not meant to be sexist. To use such notations as he/she, he or she, etc., to appear non-sexist falls short of its goal and makes the text difficult to read.

An item that can be useful in getting revenge is a complete set of false identification. This must be planned and obtained well in advance. There are many ads in paramilitary and alternate lifestyle magazines that offer false identification. However, care must be taken to insure the identification is authentic in appearance. There is no better way of drawing attention to yourself than to present a piece of questionable identification. Should this happen, abandon the project and pick it up later using another approach.

Should something go wrong, never admit to anything. Also, give careful consideration to what you tell an attorney. Attorneys are not above selling out. Offer nothing and demand all of your rights. Never admit anything, even if faced with what may appear to be overwhelming evidence. Most of it won't stand up in court unless you are stupid enough to admit something. And most of all, never plea-bargain. The deck will always be stacked against you. Plea bargains are only offered when the law comes up short with something to run with.

Later chapters in this book will depict specific actions that work well with certain institutions and people. There are also chapters on more general revenge techniques that can be used in a variety of cases.

4.
Tactics

Tactics of cold revenge are the techniques of obtaining objectives by strategies that comprise the overall plan. Tactics are the nuts and bolts of the operation, the everyday activities. The strategy may be to drive your enemy around the bend or to expose him for the fake that he is. Tactics are the means of accomplishing that goal. The tactics you may use utilize your particular expertise and the tools you have available—essentially, doing what you can with what you have. Tactics need not be earth-shaking nor original. Continual small acts can be far more effective than one grand show. Further, the small acts will draw less sympathy or reaction from the gestapo. One grand show may be spectacular, but it may create attention so that your enemy can become a martyr. In fact, he may grow from the experience. The object of cold revenge is to put your enemy down, not give him something to grow on. Single drops of water wear away great mountains.

There are a few basic rules you must follow in order to be most effective in your tactics. Like all rules, they are not written in stone. These rules emphasize that common sense must be used to select and execute your tactics. Going off on a tangent will bring disaster, something you certainly don't need when seeking cold revenge.

The first rule is never go outside your experience or expertise. That is to say, don't do anything you don't know how to do. Don't play with explosives if you haven't had experience in handling them. Don't play with explosives if you are uncomfortable around them, even if you know how to use them. This is not to say you can't learn. But bear in mind that the act of learning a new trick could lay a trail back to your doorstep. It doesn't take very much for legal institutions with their large budgets and vast resources to build a case. Why give them anything through an amateur act? Even the act of checking a book out of the library can be used against you in our present gestapo-plagued society. If you must learn a new skill to effectively carry out your plan, take great care in gaining that education. Look for books in out-of-town stores. Never buy paramilitary books near home and certainly never use a check. If you need to procure a book by mail order, use a money order and a mail drop. Mail drops can be set up through ads appearing in these magazines. Mail drops can also be set up through some of the secretarial services. This would be a good place to use false identification, putting as much space as possible between you and your operation.

The second rule is to go outside your enemy's expertise whenever possible. If there is a choice between doing something within his knowledge and something that is not, do what is alien. Pulling the sparkplug wires off a mechanic's car would have little effect beyond mild irritation, but do it at the right time to a person who doesn't know how to open the hood and the results can be far reaching. Think of the effect this would have on your enemy if it were done while he was visiting his mistress late at night. He can't leave the car there and he can't really call for help—far more than a mild irritation.

Sometime during your planning, you'll have to decide if your cold revenge strategy is to be an ongoing project or a one-shot deal. One-shot strategy carries less risk of being caught but the ongoing operations are the most effective psychologically. The one-shot strategy is like a knife stab. Ongoing operations are like turning the blade, or a death by a thousand cuts. The apparent low risk of the one-shot strategy can quickly dissolve should the act be something outrageous, and these operations usually have to be on the outrageous side to be effective. This is especially true if they are against an institution. Outrageous acts usually result in the police being called in, and if your enemy carries any clout with the local parasites, there may be an investigation. This, of course, could put you in hot water. Try to plan all your cold revenge so that it will be considered civil action should push come to shove.

If your choice is the ongoing operation, then the remaining rules should be observed. The third rule is that the anticipation and threat are far more terrifying than the actual acts. The power you obtain over an enemy through ongoing acts of cold revenge is not only what you can do, but what he thinks you can and will do. The acts themselves may be mild irritations, but having your enemy wonder when and how the next one will come can drive him around the bend. It is like an incessant stream of drops of water.

The fourth rule is to ridicule your enemy. It is almost impossible for your enemy to counter the ridicule you force on him. Ridicule works against your enemy even when you're not actively doing something. It feeds on your enemy and he will become his own worst enemy because of it. Ridicule can also force him into unwise reactions. The real action here then becomes the enemy's reaction. His friends and associates are drawn into it, and their jeering can be more effective than your action itself. An enemy properly goaded and guided in his reaction will be a major joy of cold revenge—he will be laughed at. This causes irrational anger in him that surely leads to further stupidity. A word of caution is in order here: many bullies do not play with a full deck. It can be difficult to tell just exactly what they might do. You should take precaution not to push too far or too heavily at any given time. Your well-planned strategy can quickly come to nothing if your enemy comes after you with a pistol. This is unlikely since those deserving a measure of cold revenge usually do not have that kind of courage. They seek remedies through the corrupted police and court system.

The fifth and last rule is that the tactics must be something you enjoy. If you enjoy the cold revenge you have chosen, you can keep the pressure on long enough to see a successful conclusion. If you do not enjoy what you are doing, you will make a mistake sooner or later and your enemy may become the joyful one.

5.
Timing

The most important thing to remember in applying techniques of cold revenge is timing. So important is timing, yet so often overlooked, that this chapter is dedicated to its importance. Many good plans for cold revenge come to nothing because of bad timing. For example, fouling up a bank card machine on Monday morning would be very ineffective, but try Friday evening after the bank has closed for a three-day holiday weekend. Now that shows class. Some acts of cold revenge are equally effective regardless of when they are done, but when coupled with proper timing, the result can be greatly enhanced.

It is pointless to work out a good plan only to have it fizzle because of poor timing. Any act of revenge must occur at a time when it will do the most damage to the enemy. This is a lesson often learned the hard way. Poor timing is usually the result of impatience. When a person has taken the time to assemble all the necessary items to perform an act of cold revenge, he often becomes impatient and wants to get started right away. In many cases, timing is given almost no thought at all. These cases result in minimum damage to the enemy and often the results are negative. That is why you should always plan your acts of cold revenge to take place during a time when it is most inconvenient for the enemy. Knowing your enemy's activities as well as he does insures that your timing will have the maximum effect. Even a relatively inconsequential act can cause maximum chaos if done at the right time.

Good timing is when you have the police call on your

23

enemy for an embarrassing reason when he has dinner guests, preferably his boss. You could also have it done at his place of business while important clients or customers are there. You could detach the ignition wires to his car late at night while he is visiting his mistress, or have him served with legal papers while he is being personally interviewed for a promotion.

Still don't expect much. It might prove nearly impossible to pull off some plans with the best timing, but an effort should always be made to do so. If you have a good plan, hold it until you have good timing. Better to wait a month and be really successful than to have your plan fizzle because of your impatience. This is a good example of making your revenge cold revenge. Anyone can be a trickster, and a few can become proficient enough at dirty tricks to make them work as cold revenge. But cold revenge requires that there be a goal and that it be carried out with maximum effect. Tricksters are impulsive and select their targets randomly. Usually the target is a relatively innocent person who is an easy mark. Tricksters are much like the school bully who picks on those who are weaker. Actually, they are little better than the parasites of society that the cold revenge should be aimed at. To be really proficient at cold revenge, you must have patience and consider the effect of timing in all your plans.

A lack of timing is the major cause of poor effects of otherwise well-made plans. Keep timing in mind during all phases of planning and you will find those little things you do for cold revenge take on new and greater dimensions in their effectiveness. Always ask yourself when the best time would be to take your cold revenge. As you read the chapters that follow try to think of the best time for the various tactics to be executed. Keeping timing foremost in your thoughts will truly make your cold revenge a joy.

6.
Superglue

In planning cold revenge, consider the materials available to you to carry out an effective campaign. Exotic products are usually easier to trace than simple items that can be picked up at any store. Also, the simple products are often easier to use. Along with availability, the cost of materials must be considered. It would make little sense to go broke while getting a measure of cold revenge. An easy-to-obtain and easy-to-use product that will not raise any question is superglue. Superglue is a generic term used in this book to describe the adhesives on the market today that are easy to apply, dry quickly, and display high strength. Products that require mixing do not lend themselves to the work of cold revenge. A ready-to-use product contained in a tube or a squeeze bottle with a pointed applicator or applied with a syringe is best for quick and easy application.

The great thing about superglue is that it can be obtained in hundreds of stores. Grocery stores are the best place because it can be purchased along with a large quantity of groceries. However, don't draw attention to yourself by buying too much at one time.

It doesn't take too much imagination to consider what a single drop of superglue in a lock can do. Locks and superglue just do not go together. Since locks are such an integral part of our society, it only follows that tampering with them will cause immeasurable distress. Look around you, locks are everywhere. Every device known can be locked to prevent unauthorized use. Every external door and many inside doors are fitted with locks. Every toolbox can be padlocked and file cabinets are usually fitted with a lock. Locks are truly a product of our society. Every adult has a ring of keys that controls his access to the dwellings and objects around him. Tamper with these locks and you have tampered with his life, and there is no better way to do this than with a drop of superglue. There is no limit to the amount of cold revenge that can be exacted by the use of superglue in locks.

Consider the frustration the cool Romeo will have when he returns with his latest pickup to find he can't get into his apartment because the locks are superglued. How about when the police return from shaking down some business to find they can't get into their patrol car. Or, consider how stupid the boss will look when sugerglue prevents the opening of his briefcase at an important meeting. The switches that turn on computers are often keyed locks. The office routine will surely be put into a tailspin if these were superglued. Postal meters are also locked. No postage will bring many operations to a standstill. Supergluing the locks of any place of business from a law office to a retail store, including a bank, will help make their day.

More in the line of superglue versus high tech, a small almost invisible drop of superglue on a floppy disk will soon stop the program. There is no limit to the damage that can be done to the high-tech industry. Supergluing the lock on the floppy disk file box will drive most nerds around the bend. Why? Because it's beyond their expertise and experience.

Superglue can be used in serveral ways in banks, as described in the chapter on that subject. Below are several more uses of superglue. By this time, you can no doubt see that you can wage a good war with superglue alone, and your enemy will have no real defense against these attacks. There is no way he can guard all locks, and there is no way he can eliminate them.

Peace and quiet can be had from the roar of motorcycles with a drop of superglue in the ignition lock. Superglue in your enemy's post office box lock will give him some anxious moments. The phone company will really love you for supergluing the locks on their coin boxes. Supergluing the locks on the display cases in stores will bring a halt to sales for a while. A drop of superglue in the ignition of a school bus will prevent a normal day at school. The neighbor who walks his dog on your lawn will have a moment to reflect while the locksmith figures out how to get around that single drop of superglue in his door lock.

Any lock makes a good target for superglue, but none gives more satisfaction than those of governmental agencies. There is no limit to the number of ways these petty gestapo agents can be harassed with superglued locks. One of the best is supergluing the locks on the courtroom doors during the noon recess. Everyone has to enter the courtroom through the judge's chamber. This takes a touch of class to pull off.

Superglue can be used in far more applications than in just locks. Consider the results of supergluing a telephone to its base, or a windshield wiper to the windshield. How about supergluing the door to the jamb? A drop of superglue on the base threads of a burned-out light bulb in its socket will make the apartment manager regret not returning a deposit. The same is true with supergluing windows, light switches, thermostat controls, and many other moveable items. Supergluing a single paper clip to a parasite's desk will surely ruin his day. Imagination is all it takes to use superglue.

Then there was the restaurant that poisoned several customers through the sloppy handling of food. One victim returned and superglued all the glasses, dishes, and silverware to the table during rush hour. Here is a case where timing is very important. Supergluing cans and jars to the shelves in supermarkets can be annoying too. Timing isn't so important here, but late in the day is the best time to allow it to set up overnight. This, of course, suggests supergluing everything down to some deserving bastard's desk. This works best when done to an expensive wood desk.

Another classic was done by a person not even employed by the county. He superglued the pages of often-used reference books in the county clerk's office. The same person superglued all the microfiche together in the county assessor's office.

A few drops of superglue on a coin going into a parking meter will gum up the mechanism. Meters that still take pennies are cheap to screw up. Fifty cents will almost put a small town out of business. These same tactics apply to all coin-operated machines. Remember your planning and timing when undertaking these campaigns.

Although your cold revenge operation cannot be based entirely on the use of superglue, it can bring about a lot of harassment, which may be all that is needed to drive your enemy around the bend and make him react irrationally. A good tactic is to hit your enemy very heavy with superglue for a time, then switch to something else. You can then go back to the superglue routine later, which will shock him since he knows what lies ahead.

Superglue is one of the cheapest and most useful items you can have in your cold revenge toolbox. Its uses are limited only by the imagination of the user. Buy a few tubes and keep them handy. The opportunities to use superglue are always presenting themselves in the strangest ways. Many of these opportunities do not repeat themselves—be prepared, don't leave home without it.

7.
Motor Oil and Other Goodies

There isn't an item or substance that cannot be used to bring about some measure of cold revenge. In selecting things to use in your quest for cold revenge, keep in mind that the more exotic a product, the easier it can be traced. Your arsenal should be limited to things that are easy to procure and impossible to trace. Even if it can be shown that you procured a common item or product, it doesn't implicate you in an act of cold revenge.

One common product that works very well in many applications is motor oil, new or used. Used motor oil works best in fouling things up because of the high content of burned carbon. New motor oil contains a lot of detergent and sometimes washes completely out of fabric. Stains from used motor oil are nearly impossible to wash out. New motor oil can be purchased almost anywhere without drawing attention. Used motor oil is usually free, but it is best if you use motor oil from your own car. Collecting used motor oil from service stations will surely draw attention. If in doubt about whether the source of your used motor oil can be traced, forget it and use new motor oil. The common brands that are widely available are your best choice. If the can is left behind be sure to wear gloves and leave no fingerprints.

One of the most effective uses of motor oil is in swimming pools. Here it makes little difference if it is new or used. Motor oil in a swimming pool will put it out of commission for several days, even weeks, and in some cases for the entire season. This is an excellent act to use on an apartment building landlord, where your damage deposit was not returned. Granted, this may be inconvenient to other tenants, but if they were clods and had been bothering you with loud music and motorcycles, then you are getting a lot for your efforts. Remember your timing. Motor oil in the swimming pool the night before the fourth of July weekend is far more effective than the day after.

Another place where motor oil causes problems is in washers and dryers. In this case, used motor oil works best. Try this if you want to drive the apartment manager around the bend. If you really want to mess up an apartment, spray used motor oil all over the carpet, walls, ceiling, drapes, bath, etc. If the apartment is furnished, pour a generous amount on the mattress and the furniture covered with fabric. This along with rotting fish in the disconnected refrigerator and superglue in the locks should make someone's day.

The uses of motor oil in getting cold revenge are as unlimited as those of superglue. Between these two easily obtained items, you can make all the trouble your enemy can handle. To help your imagination along, think about the effect of used motor oil on your enemy's new sheepskin seat covers in his car, or a quart on your boss's desk. Again, remember timing can make things even worse. Applying used motor oil on the sheepskin seat covers while your enemy is dining out with his date or mistress will certainly put a crimp on the sexual activities he had planned for later that evening. It will also cause him to be so outraged that he will make a complete ass of himself.

Sometimes you may not wish to cause permanent damage. In that case, good substitutes for motor oil are molasses or syrup. These are more expensive to obtain but will wash out far easier than used motor oil.

If you want to leave a lasting impression on the fabric of a couch or expensive seat in an automobile, use ink. The type used in stamp pads is very effective and will not wash out easily, if at all. If you have been screwed over by an auto dealer, this is a very good tactic. A few bottles of stamp pad ink will mess up every car in the showroom. Do this before a busy weekend of car sales.

An easy-to-obtain product that can be used effectively

against shopping centers and other institutions is nails. A few pounds of roofing nails scattered around the parking lot will dampen an expensive weekend sales promotion. Roofing nails and parking lots just don't mix. If it's a graveled lot, the effect is tenfold since they can't be swept away. Broken glass can have a similar effect. Don't break the bottles on the parking lot or you will draw attention.

A chemical product that can be most useful is butyric acid. A small amount of it will stink up an area badly. Leaving small bottles where they will be knocked over can be a calling card your enemy won't forget soon. Its use is ideal in offices catering to the public, from a doctor's office to the mayor's. Butyric acid will also stink up a bank, law office, post office, police station, movie theater, supermarket, and most other places that are relatively enclosed. One of the best places to do your number with butyric acid is in courtrooms. There is no better place to perform your acts of cold revenge than in the tabernacle of the scum and parasites who through their greed and corruption have made cold revenge necessary.

The procurement of illegal drugs can be very dangerous, and unless the soft underbelly of your enemy is dope and your plan is to have him busted, they will serve little purpose. It is recommended that you stay away from drugs in your plans for cold revenge.

Many additives can be useful in getting a measure of cold revenge; however, many of them are as dangerous to the user as to the enemy. Unless you are well educated with additives, you should give serious consideration to their use. Those that are meant to be put in your enemy's food or drink may have serious consequences. Unless you plan to kill your enemy, it is best to stay away from these chancy products.

An often-overlooked product is everyday paint. A gallon, or even a quart, of cheap house paint dumped on your enemy's car will make him know you were there. Paint can also be used in much the same way as motor oil and can often be more effective. Motor oil can be washed off or out whereas paint cannot. Paint can be put into spherical Christmas tree decorations with a bit of modeling clay to seal the opening to make a bomb that can easily be thrown. Handle them with care—

they can break in your pocket. Spray paint can be useful provided the nozzle doesn't clog at the wrong time.

Even common items such as motor oil should be purchased away from where you live. Common sense and caution will go a long way in keeping you out of trouble. Again, as you gather these supplies and take your revenge, the urge to share this excitement will become overpowering. The police count on this characteristic to solve many of their cases. So keep your own counsel and your mouth shut. Share your moments of glory with someone twenty years later.

8.
Telephones

Of all the inventions that have invaded our lives, the telephone is one of the least dispensable. The telephone has become a tool for all occasions. Being such an instrument, it is looked upon with mixed feelings. Like a double-edged sword, the telephone can cut both ways.

The telephone has become so common that it must be looked upon as both an instrument and an institution. The telephone as an instrument is a very handy tool. It can save thousands of hours and many miles of travel in doing your work. As an institution, the telephone is a quasi-governmental bully. In the past this bully was generally referred to as "Ma Bell." This is no longer the case, but the quasi-governmental bully is still there.

The telephone company itself is more often enemy than not. It is a fact that the telephone companies rate high on almost everyone's list as one of the most deserving of cold revenge. Their employees take on quasi-bureaucratic airs that make even government employees look human. Even petty civil servants who usually rate a good measure of cold revenge seek revenge against the telephone companies. Stealing service from the telephone companies is common by anyone who thinks he can get away with it. There was a belief that the AT&T breakup would cure some of these problems. It hasn't. If anything, things have gotten worse. Now every little two-bit telephone company has its own little empire and lets everyone know it. Rates continue to rise and service continues to decline. These newly created empires won't even give you the time of day without charging extra for the call.

Since the telephone is both a tool for cold revenge as well as an enemy upon which you may want to bestow it, it is necessary to separate the two issues. The case of perpetrating cold revenge on the telephone company will be discussed first.

One way to begin on this task is to superglue everything owned by the telephone company—the coin-box lock on pay phones, the handsets to the cradle on pay phones, the locks on the phone company's offices and trucks, and anything else that looks like it would hamper operations if made fast to another object. If supergluing everything the telephone company has its name on seems too tame, there are other things you can do. Disconnect the two wires leading into the phone and connect them to a 120 volt supply. This will give the phone company some real headaches. Among the tamer things you can do is to call them and request new service to a vacant house or lot. This, of course, will have little overall effect and is harassment at best.

A much more effective way of getting back at the telephone companies is to run up high long-distance calls for which you have no intention of paying. This can be done in several ways. The easiest, of course, is on your own phone when you are about to move out of the area. However, you should take the telephone service out in a different name in the first place. This requires advanced planning. False identification would come in handy. It has been recommended that such service always be taken out in another name to allow for anonymity.

Another method of running up long-distance charges is to have them charged to another number. If this happens to belong to the enemy, then you are getting two for the price of one. The practice of putting test jacks on the outside of buildings on new installations makes for easy rip-off of the phone company's service. The owner of the phone you tapped into will not have to pay for these calls unless he is some kind of fool. If he is, don't worry about it. An even better idea would be to tap into a telephone company's employee's private phone. They deserve each other.

The telephone companies being licensed by the FCC enjoy the protection of the federal government. Is it any wonder our taxes are so high? Every half-baked and greedy parasite is in some way protected by the Feds. This must be borne in mind when working out your strategy against the telephone companies. Because of this protection the only way to really get to the telephone companies is through nonpayment of service or destruction of equipment. Another way is to disrupt service. This latter choice, however, can affect many innocent people. The purpose of cold revenge is not to cause undue hardship on innocent people, since they often can be drawn into a force against the enemy. However, when innocent people are unduly inconvenienced they are driven to the side of the enemy. They do not see that your acts are against the enemy, but their own inconvenience. They fail to recognize that what you are doing is really on their behalf in the long run. Therefore, action against the telephone companies should be directed toward the company as an entity rather than their service.

Because the telephone is a useful tool in exacting cold revenge on your enemy, you would not want to wreck the system. Even if your enemy is the telephone company. The telephone should not be used to make threatening calls as it can be put to much better use. Besides, there is no way you can really punch your enemy out over the phone. You can only collect and disseminate thoughts over the phone.

One of the best uses for the telephone is gathering information about your enemy. People employed by government agencies, banks, and other quasi-public institutions usually suffer advanced cases of diarrhea of the mouth. They must tell all that they know to show how important they are. If you want to know how much money your enemy has in the bank, just call his bank and ask them. They'll be happy to tell you. It gives them a sense of importance. However, if you went to a teller in person, you would not get this information so easily. It's strange how you can get information over the phone.

If getting information over the phone is easy, giving information is even easier. That is, false information. Consider the chaos you can cause by calling the enemy's wife just before he plans to leave on a business trip. Pretend to be from the airline and tell her that her husband can pick up his two tickets for whatever romantic place the "in" people are going to. Then sit back and watch the fireworks. A little imagination can lead to hundreds of variations of this scenario.

Another thing you can do with the telephone is to report your enemy's car as stolen. Timing is important here. A good time is when your enemy has some important visitors he is showing around. To add to the effect, do it just after they have had lunch and are likely to have liquor on their breaths. With a little luck, your enemy might not be able to pass the blood-alcohol test. You can even call the newspaper to report your enemy has been arrested for some weird crime. This doesn't always work since most newspapers double-check this kind of information, but there are lazy reporters that might print it. There is no limit to passing false information over the telephone. It is surprising the far-reaching effect these acts can have. A seed of deceit can grow into a very large can of worms.

Other uses of the telephone are to have anything from a load of gravel to five cords of firewood, or a couple of yards of manure delivered to your enemy and dumped on his driveway. Again, timing is important. The manure will be far more effective if delivered the day of the evening your enemy plans to have a party. Even if he manages to get rid of it, the smell will linger for days. All kinds of services and products can be ordered for your enemy by phone. Spacing these orders over several weeks or months will be most effective in driving your enemy around the bend. Doing this can be greatly enhanced if you get your enemy's credit card numbers while you gather information about him. Many places will accept telephone orders with an oral credit card number.

Although the telephone companies are one of the most deserving organizations for receiving cold revenge, they provide the telephone which is one of the best tools in your arsenal for exacting cold revenge. Treat it as such and it will serve you well. Because the telephone is such a great tool, you might even be able to forgive, for a time, the jerks who run the telephone companies. Let your fingers do your walking when spreading false information or gathering information about your enemy. The telephone can save hours of driving and greatly speed up the process of getting that full measure of cold revenge.

9.
Banks

It is doubtful that there could be a universal bunch of parasites on this planet more deserving of a full measure of cold revenge than banks. Banks do more things to screw up the lives of more people than any other institution. It is indeed rare to find anyone who has not had a serious difference of opinion with a bank. Their sickeningly self-righteous and pious attitude causes even the most benevolent person to have doubts not only about the system but about the whole human race. Because banks for the most part, are insured and regulated by the federal government, any act of revenge against them becomes a federal case. It is precisely this protection that has made the banks the way they are. Even padding a net worth statement is a crime if you present it to a bank to obtain a loan. The banks are so well protected that even raising your voice in anger can result in arrest. You never find anyone worth anything working for a bank for very long. Bankers, too, are corrupt. This explains why so many banks have made bad loans and are going under holding up innocent citizens' funds by allowing only small withdrawals each month. Considering the lowness that banks have sunk to, it is clear they fully deserve anything they get.

Because they are so well protected, one must be ingenious and careful to achieve revenge against these petty parasites. Seeking revenge against banks is one of the rare occasions where false identification can be used. The identification will have to be well planned because the banks carefully check these things out. The effort needed to secure good false identification will be well worth the time. It is time that people stand up among the few and tell the banks they have been dumped on enough.

Revenge against a bank almost certainly has to be cold to succeed without your being caught. The timing works out well since it takes time to get the false identification and establish rapport before tripping the trap. It is best to pull your revenge tactics at a branch where you are not known, preferably out of town. Some banks do not have branches so you have to find some way to work around that. Contact with the out-of-town branch should be done by mail only, except for opening an account or safe deposit box. Mail must be returned to an address other than your own, preferably a post office box or mail drop. Do nothing that will attract attention or cause someone to remember you. Remember to keep your own counsel and share nothing with anyone.

One of the first things you can do to a bank is to gum-up its automatic teller machines. There are many ways of doing this including shoving dog shit into the card slot or feeding in a card coated with superglue. Do this to all the bank's branches in a wide area at the same time (for example, the first evening of a long holiday weekend). This little trick doesn't require anything other than plastic cards and glue. Another trick you might consider is spreading roofing nails around the parking area used by bank customers. Nails in any part of the bank's parking lot will give them something to think about, but spread around the automatic teller machine will have the most satisfying results.

If the above sounds too tame, try the often-used fish in the safe deposit box. Remember, there are other things than fish that will cause equal distress to a bank manager. Canta-loupe is a good product for a lasting smell, but not as good as fish, which is hard to beat. Also, try putting some superglue on the bottom of the box. They'll have a near impossible time getting the box out even after they drill the lock. Some banks will leave you alone in the vault with your box. Put some superglue in some of the other locks while you're there. This will cause years of grief for the bank because some people seldom open their safe deposit boxes.

If you are careful in keeping a low profile and use   good

false identification when renting the safe deposit box, you can place the noxious substance in it, glue its bottom and all the locks in the vault, and still enjoy a good measure of revenge without detection. Do this to several branches at the same time and your revenge will multiply beyond your wildest dreams. Want just a little revenge in between acts? Make up some rolls of coins with a drop of superglue between each coin. You can also superglue the pens to the writing desks in the lobby of the bank.

Another way to make a bank regret the day it fouled you up is to get a key to the night deposit vault. It is easy to imagine the unlimited things that can be done here—anything from dog shit to hot coals will really make some banker's day. Getting a key to the night deposit vault will probably require that you open up a business account with that branch. Be sure your false identification is in order and wait several months before you act.

If more serious revenge is sought, there is no end to the nightmares you can cause with a few phony accounts writing and depositing checks on each other. With a lot of checks moving among three or four accounts, the bank will waste lots of time trying to determine what is really happening. You might even get some of their large accounts involved in this scam. To open these accounts, you will need a good set of false identification. Don't do this under your own name, and open each account at a different branch. To do this correctly you should have a different set of false identification for each account. It's a lot of trouble but the end results are worth the effort.

Banks are hard to get at with many of the usual cold revenge tactics. They are also protected by the federal government. It may make more sense to go after the individual who caused you problems than the bank itself. All you can really do is chip around the edges, but this may be enough. How do you let the bank know it was you that gave them all the trouble? Don't be too quick to claim the glory. It will dawn on them sooner or later. You may even have to stand in line with others wanting to take credit for your acts.

10.
Utilities

Utility companies, such as electric, gas, water, and sewer, are sources of irritation much the same as telephone companies. The people who work for them often have that quasi-government employee attitude where they don't care. This is probably true—they don't have to care. They have monopoly on the service they provide and the customer has no choice. These utilities are so much a part of our lives now that we cannot function without them. Since the utility companies have a monopoly in their area of service, it makes it very difficult when troubles are encountered. This, along with the fact that they can discontinue their service, makes them quasi-governmental in nature. Anything you do to obtain cold revenge against a utility, public or private, will be met with maximum investigation. Bearing this in mind, you must leave no trail behind you.

Many of these utility companies have recognized that they are vulnerable to attacks of revenge. To counter this they have stepped up their public relations activities and some have even added consumer advocates to their staff. This really does not do the consumer any good. It is designed to pacify the consumer, reduce the chance of attack, and head off class action suits against them. Class action suits are becoming more and more common in states where younger and more liberal people are taking office. This action against a utility has little or no success in conservative states where corruption is prevalent.

What, you might ask, can be done to these companies to obtain a measure of cold revenge? Not all that much. Destruction of equipment such as shooting holes into transformers is a common method of destroying the electric utility's property. This can be done in rural areas with little risk of being caught. In fact, a well-planned operation can easily net twenty-five or more transformers before the gestapo or the electric company can get out to a rural area to see what happened. An operation like this requires a lot of planning and the knowledge of exactly where every transformer to be hit is located.

Another sport is to shoot the insulators on the high tension lines. An even more severe action is to bring down one of their transmission towers. All of these things are feasible through proper planning and timing.

Smashing power meters on vacation homes will keep the electric companies very busy if the timing is right. Do it after the routine meter reading and just before a long holiday weekend. Several meters in a large area will keep them busy and create a lot of bad feelings against the utility. This takes a lot of planning since you must know where all the vacation homes are in a given utility's district. Not fair to the people who own the vacation homes? A joke. These people are the ones who work for these quasi-government organizations or other businesses that specialize in ripping off and dumping on the public. How many working stiffs do you know who own vacation homes? Don't worry about it. They get those second homes by dumping on people like you.

Natural gas companies are much more difficult to get at. In general, they are far more deserving of a measure of cold revenge than their electric brothers. Gas equipment, for the most part, is buried in the ground. This requires far greater effort to cause damage, but it also takes more effort for the company to find and repair the damage. Obviously, the idea here is to cut the line. This can be dangerous, but with some planning, the line can be cut, plugged, and the damage section covered so it will take hours before it is discovered. If you're lucky, it may take days. Don't do this in the winter—there is nothing to be gained by freezing innocent people. That's a gas company's specialty.

The best way to get revenge on the utility companies is through destruction of their equipment, but this takes planning to be effective. Their property is usually difficult to get to and most acts will draw considerable investigation from all levels of law enforcement. There are, however, small acts that can be effective if used ongoingly. Among these, of course, is the planned use of superglue. All utility companies have trucks, which are locked most of the time. Superglue in the door locks will certainly wreck their schedule. Many utility companies have collection boxes to make payments after hours. These make excellent places to deposit refuse and other undesirable items. There is always the nails-in-the-parking-lot number. Another thing that can cause them a lot of grief is to request service to vacant houses or lots.

Meter tampering is another effective measure. This is a serious violation that is almost always discovered. It is strongly recommended that you do not do it to your own meter; however, meter tampering should not be overlooked as a tool for cold revenge. Consider the results of tampering with your enemy's meter and then reporting it to the utility company.

Meters are easy to tamper with and there are several handbooks available telling you how it's done. If you don't want to go this far, you can be effective by cutting the seal on your enemy's meter and reporting that he is tampering with his meter. The end result will be much the same as if he actually tampered with it himself. In any event, think of the embarrassment it will cause one way or the other.

For the true advocate of cold revenge, there is one trick that will cause someone a lot of extra work and may even involve a utility, especially an electric utility, in vast time-consuming lawsuits. You have to follow the activities of the utility very closely and when you learn of a new transmission line or other project going in, watch the site. When the surveyors have done their work, change their stake locations. You can put the project hundreds of feet off. This will be sufficient to put them outside of their right-of-way. Believe it or not, no one will say anything to the utility until the project is finished. Then the surveyors are all over the place and certain land suddenly increases in value. Sound like a lot of work? It is, but almost anything worthwhile usually is. By the way, it is always a good idea to pull up any survey stakes you come across. Make it as difficult as possible to rape the land.

Although the examples shown here are directed toward electric and gas utilities, the same techniques can work equally well on the water company. There are a few things you can do to a water district that usually cause total chaos. Contaminating reservoirs is an excellent example. However, never use a contaminant that is really dangerous. There are too many innocent people involved. Try something simple like food coloring. Remember, *you are seeking cold revenge—not carrying out terrorist activites.*

These few ideas along with whatever you can imagine will most likely satisfy the need for revenge against these quasi-government parasites of society. But it is wise to keep in mind that many of the problems encountered with utility companies are caused by some petty individual, usually a newly appointed supervisor or a newly hired hotshot, who feels the need to exert his authority. Wouldn't it be better to go after him? How about actually tampering with *his* meter? Now that would show a touch of real class.

11.
Printing

Printed material can be an extremely effective tool in getting cold revenge on your enemy. On the surface this may not appear too exciting. After all, what can the printed word really do to your enemy? Physically, nothing. In fact, there is little in this book that will help if you are seeking to bestow physical punishment. From a psychological point of view, there is probably no better tool than the written word. People tend to believe what is written far more than what is spoken. Many people say things they would never consider putting in writing. People say things which they consider to be "off the record." If they won't speak for the record, they certainly wouldn't write what they think. With this in mind, the person who puts what he has to say into writing is usually believed. It is just one of those things.

Regardless of what people may say, they are certainly concerned about what other people think of them. This is especially true with the bullies and parasites of our society. The idea of what others think of us has been driven into us from our first day on this planet. We are always expected to impress others of our importance, our charm, and a dozen other attributes of our personality; our job, our place in society, and our place in the hereafter. Knowing this, you can use the written word very effectively to at least give the appearance of forming a negative public opinion of your enemy.

Things that you must guard against in using the written word as cold revenge are the accusation of libel and the criminal charge of threatening. Never put a threat into writing. It not only marks you as an amateur, but is a very good thing for the gestapo to use to put you out of circulation for a while. In some courts, a threat will draw a heavier sentence than a committed act. This is probably because the mental anguish is more than the bullies and parasites of the world can handle. Knowing this will put you in a league far ahead of your enemy.

Libel is the act of putting something in writing that is both not true and damaging to your enemy. Note that the statement must not only be untrue but also damaging. In order to be libel, your enemy must in some way be damaged. If you say that your enemy is a nice guy when he obviously isn't, there would be no libel because he is not damaged by the statement. That is why a deceased person cannot have libel committed against him. If you intend to use the written word as a tool against your enemy, especially if it is made public, it is suggested that you study up on libel laws and have a good understanding of them. Also, understand what is meant by invasion of privacy. What you make public in writing about your enemy may be absolutely true, but it may be an invasion of his privacy, which can put you in as much hot water as if you had written lies about him. An example would be that if your enemy were taking treatments for herpes and you put that in writing, it would not be libel but could be considered as an invasion of privacy. Libel is an issue of truth versus falsehood, and is damaging. Invasion of privacy, on the other hand, is a more subjective judgment. And the same judgment is not valid for everyone, i.e., people in the public eye have less right to privacy than a low-keyed individual who has no political or public associations. What constitutes invasion of privacy varies from state to state and from judge to judge. Knowing this should not keep you from using the written word as a tool for cold revenge, but should make you consider *what* you put into writing.

One of the simplest ways to use the written word as a tool of cold revenge is to spread false information. If your enemy just returned from a business trip or even a hunting trip with the boys, you may want to make it look like he was somewhere else. You could send a letter on scented, feminine stationery to his home. In the letter, you could say what a wonderful time you had on his recent visit. Your imagination can fill in the blanks. False information in letter form can be very devastating, and when done on an ongoing basis, can drive your enemy around the bend. This is not libel or invasion of privacy. It is just false information.

Putting the truth in writing can be equally devastating, as in the example of whistle blowing. Letting someone in authority know that a petty parasite is out of line is indeed a very good act of cold revenge. Letting your department head know that your enemy has been stealing office supplies is a good example of whistle blowing. There isn't a bully or parasite in society who doesn't have his hand in the cookie jar in one way or another. Look for these opportunities and make the best of them. Whistle blowing has become respectable in the last few years because people have learned there is no honor in protecting petty scum and parasites. When you see a wrong, it is your responsibility to speak out.

The written word can work through the use of innuendo. An excellent example is using an envelope with a return address such as the county health department, and the words clearly printed in large letters, HERPES TEST RESULTS. This sent to your enemy at work will certainly give him cause to wonder what those who saw his mail may think. Remember, being a bully, he is concerned what others think. Timing here can be important: have these letters delivered while he is on vacation. Be sure to put several sheets of paper in the envelope to give it bulk, and the printed words PERSONAL AND CONFIDENTIAL on the envelope.

There are unlimited variations to what you can do with the return address on an envelope. Most important, it should draw attention and cause doubt or curiosity. Just a few examples are: AIDS TEST RESULTS, PROBATION OFFICER, PRISONER WORK RELEASE PROGRAM, CHILD ABUSE CENTER, WIFE BEATERS ANONYMOUS, and KLEPTO-MANIAC CENTER. These must be professional looking and must follow some official state, county, or city department title. Such departments need not exist, but can be generic in nature. Envelopes from state, county, or city departments can be easily obtained, and with transfer lettering and paste-ups you can do a good job, which can be copied onto envelopes on any copy machine. Also bear in mind that the use of innuendo must be something current and distasteful to the majority of the population. An innuendo about polio will fall flat. An innuendo about social diseases, drinking or drugs, and wife or child beating will give you the effect you desire.

Other forms of the printed word can be displayed on bumper stickers, decals, badges, and a host of other public display items. A good idea for a bumper sticker is the name of the auto dealer followed by the words, AUTO REPAIR FRAUD. The things that can be said about businesses are unlimited. Remember the Bell Telephone classic? The Bell trademark followed by, WE DON'T CARE, WE DON'T HAVE TO. It might have contributed to the break-up of that parasitic operation. Look around, you'll see endless opportunities to use bumper stickers and the like to help your revenge. It is even acceptable to use four letter words on bumper stickers. However, the use of them takes away a degree of credibility from the message. Try to stay a little above the gutter and your message will have more impact.

It is only fitting to point out that the printed word is a vivid example of the pen being mightier than the sword. Remember this, and pen and paper may be the only things you need to exact your cold revenge.

12.
Classified Ads

At first glance, classified advertisement does not appear to be a useful tool in cold revenge. It appears to be merely an extension of the printed word. To some extent this is true, but this chapter highlights the unique ways classified ads can spread false information and create doubt. In other forms of the written word, such as letters, the aim is usually toward one person, whereas the classified ad is aimed at the masses, in much the same way as the bumper sticker.

Classified ads as a tool for cold revenge may be short-lived. Once your enemy finds out about these ads, he can quickly have them stopped. To ensure that your effort has maximum effect, plan your ads with great care and be sure to consider timing. With proper timing, you will not have to keep your ad running for a long period of time. Your cold revenge can be achieved by the ad running one day.

Classified ads can be printed in newspapers as well as magazines. The cost is less in newspapers, but ads in magazines have a wider readership. Classified ads in newspapers are often overlooked unless someone is looking for a specific item. Even then, your ad is likely to be overlooked in the larger daily papers. In small town weeklies your ad has a better chance of being seen. You should consider whether the people you want to see the ad read the publication you intend to use.

Using classified ads to put out false information is usually accomplished in a left-handed manner. This will help you to effectively plan your ad campaign. An effective ad is one that starts something like a rumor mill. When this is done correctly, it matters little who actually reads the ad. Ads listing your enemy's house for sale might well give the impression that he is moving. This may be the opposite of what he needs if he wants the image of stability. To get an even better effect with such an ad, include words such as LEAVING STATE, MUST SELL. Of course, your enemy's name will have to appear to have maximum effect. This type of ad can be used with almost any piece of property, but the effect you want depends largely on timing.

Another use of the classified ad is to instill doubt. Such ads as notices of not being responsible for any debts other than his own often appear when a divorce is in progress. These ads, which appear in the personal section, are always read by financial institutions who follow these announcements very carefully. This can create doubt and can wreck your enemy's credit for several months. Use this one when you know your enemy is trying to borrow money and sit back and watch the fun when he gets rejected.

Although the classified ad can be effective in creating false information and doubt, its best use is sometimes in simple harassment. The things that can be done with the classified ad to harass your enemy are almost unlimited. This type of ad must be designed so that dozens or even hundreds of people take some action that will greatly annoy your enemy. A good example is that if your enemy is an employer, an unwanted help-wanted ad will give him a headache if the timing is right. Know when your enemy is least likely to want telephone calls or when your enemy is the busiest. Have the prospective employees call on him in person at that time. Either of these cases will drive him around the bend. Keep up the pressure and run the ad several weeks. If your enemy is in the process of laying off employees, a help-wanted ad will completely undermine the morale of the employees he wishes to retain. If your enemy deals some product, make the ad read of some super bargain, or better still that he will buy as much of that product as he can get at a well-above market price. Granted, your enemy doesn't have to buy or sell, but his reputation will be damaged, and isn't that what you are really after? This is the type of act that makes cold revenge worth waiting and planning for.

The harassment created by advertising a garage sale at your enemy's house, or having strangers call at all hours of the night, are a lot of playful fun, but normally short-lived and have no lasting effect. However, if your enemy is high strung and any disorder in his life sets him off, by all means use small harassment ads and let him self-destruct. To see one of these parasites of society destroy himself over petty harassment is a joy in itself. Indeed, to watch any of these slugs and parasites of society self-destruct under any condition is a joy.

Classified ads can be taken a step further into what are commonly called display ads. Display ads can take on the look of an offical public announcement. In it you might make some announcement that will put your enemy in a bad light. A good example of this was done by myself a few years ago. Having had trouble with a printer over a contract to print a book, a one-column wide display ad was run in the paper. Its heading said PUBLIC NOTICE. This was followed by a request that anyone having trouble of any kind with that printer should call a number and ask for me. Believe it or not, many calls were received and the printer's business slipped enough that his attorney made a lot of noise. The steady pressure rendered the printer a nonentity in his business. Another sharp downturn in the economy would wipe him out. It can't be said that this display ad was the sole cause, but it certainly was another nail in his box that woke the public to his shoddy operation. Later in the same city, a fired legal secretary used a similar ad to request former employees to come forward and tell of the sexual harassment they received while working for the law firm that fired her. Being a small town, the effect put the integrity of the firm on the line.

Classified and display ads are not restricted to newspapers and magazines. The same type of ad can be typed out on index cards and posted on bulletin boards at supermarkets, shopping centers, recreational areas, and churches. Most churches also have newsletters where, for a small fee, you can place ads and other commercial announcements. If you can manage to get an announcement in one of these, especially if it is your enemy's own church, you will certainly have made his day. Many times the newspaper won't take an ad because it feels it may be sued or it considers the ad to be in poor taste. Your enemy may be a friend of the editor or publisher, or perhaps a large advertiser in that paper. Remember, parasites who are deserving of cold revenge are also the type who cultivate associations with many sources.

These simple classified and display ads can have far-reaching effects if carefully worded and published at the right time. They usually work best in smaller newspapers. Study the ad section in your local paper and see where you can fit your ad to help you along that path of giving your enemy a taste of the cold revenge he deserves.

13.
Supermarkets and Retail Stores

The burning desire for cold revenge against supermarkets and other retail stores arises often enough that the methods used against them should be well thought out. Naturally, each type of store requires a different line of action. Action against retail stores must be aimed at disrupting service to drive customers away. The public is generally very sensitive to stores that are having problems and tends to stay away from them. They are afraid that the problems will rub off on them. It follows that almost anything you do to a retail store will drive away customers. If you can drive enough away, you can put the store out of business. This may take time, but the result will be well worth the effort. In studying retail stores, you soon discover that some fall into categories that lend themselves to a fixed type of revenge. Other stores, because of their size or location, require tailor-made action. However, certain acts lend themselves to virtually every type of retail store. Among these are the superglue in the locks and nails in the parking lot routines. Not being able to open the doors in the morning could be all that is needed to make someone's day. Doing just these two things on the eve of a big sale could pay a little interest to your joy of cold revenge.

Of all the various stores, supermarkets lend themselves to the widest and easiest acts of harassment. When one stops to think, there are hundreds of nasty things a person can do to a supermarket. To begin with, a loaded grocery cart packed with frozen foods and ice cream abandoned on a very busy day will not be noticed for hours. By then the damage is done.

Why not put a carton of ice cream behind some cereal boxes in the cereal display? If ice cream seems too tame, try a punctured can of motor oil or even a bottle of vegetable oil. Think of the different sections in a supermarket and how you can best disrupt that section. Rigging egg cartons so a stack of them will topple over is a classic. This is a variation on upsetting a pyramid of cans, but is even more effective. A small hole in a gallon milk carton can make a nice mess. In fact, a small hole in almost any container of liquid makes a mess. For dry items such as laundry soap, use a razor blade or utility knife to slice along the bottom of the carton. A package of fish hidden away behind some canned goods near closing time will not be noticed until the next morning. Then it really will be noticed!

The above examples should be enough to keep anyone busy for some time. But let's consider a few more ideas. Cut the bottom of a few ten-pound bags of potatoes and watch the fun when the spuds hit the deck. Open up a can of sardines just before closing time to give the place a nice smell in the morning. Or open a can or two of several six-packs of beer or pop. And the latest classic: a dead rat placed in one of the bulk food containers.

The drugstores of today are much the same as supermarkets. In fact, many drugstores now have aisles of food products. The same acts of cold revenge that work against supermarkets will work against the drugstore. The addition of departments such as sporting goods and fabrics lends a few other ideas to consider. Fabrics can be ruined beyond use by pouring motor oil on them. A bottle of ink will also do well. Since the fabrics are stacked on tables, it is easy to puncture a can of motor oil and bury it among them. When you purchase the motor oil or ink from the same drugstore, the damage is a double treat.

Sporting goods departments lend themselves to several revenge techniques. Puncturing the basketballs, or setting up boxes of fishhooks so they spill on the floor always gets the attention of the store manager. If the store sells shot for shotgun shell reloading, cut open a couple of bags in such a way that they won't spill until they are moved. The twenty-five pound bags of number eight shot contain tens of thousands of shot that will be around for a very long time. Another act that will scare the hell out of the punks is to load a blank in the tube magazine of a lever action rifle. *Never* use anything other than a blank. You can never tell where a round might go. A blank will more than do the job. This act will usually get the sporting goods manager fired — a perfect act if he is your enemy.

One word of caution about drugstores is to never under any circumstances do anything to a drug product. This warrants repeating: Never do anything to any drug product. It is a terrorist act and has no place in the arsenal of cold revenge. Anyone who tampers with any drug products deserves anything that happens to him.

Furniture stores are often the worthy recipients of cold revenge. Some of the junk they sell that falls apart shortly after delivery is sufficient motive to declare war. The store is never responsible, it seems. You have to deal with the manufacturer at the other end of the country. Cold revenge is certainly in order when you spend hundreds of dollars on a piece of furniture that comes unglued or falls apart shortly after delivery. A utility knife run along the side of a few sofas or chairs should let them know how you feel. Motor oil is also good, but you may have trouble getting it into the store. A small bottle of ink will do as well and is easier to carry in. Scratching the tops of tables and other finished wooden furniture can be great sport for you, but not for them. Time your acts during the first hours of a sale for best results.

Department stores offer endless opportunities for getting even. Revenge should be directed toward the department or individual that caused you damage. Act while that person is on shift—lay the blame where it belongs. This will, however, expose you to greater risk especially if you complained and were unsatisfied. If you made a lot of noise, better to delay your cold revenge until the smoke has cleared. Even then some people have long memories: be cautious.

In stores that have television and stereo departments, superglue will probably be your best friend. A few drops on the controls will render a unit worthless. Also remember that speakers are easily damaged or destroyed. How? Reverse the wires on them, or use a long sharp instrument to puncture the diaphragms. And paint on a picture tube doesn't add to the quality of the picture.

Another way to get at retail stores is to sucker them into making a false arrest for shoplifting. Make them think you stole something that you took into the store in the first place. This can be very tricky and is definitely not for the faint of heart. One good example is accomplished with a new tape measure. Purchase the tape measure from one store and get a receipt showing the item and price paid. Then pull the tape all the way out and put the owner's name on the bottom of the tape with a marker pen. Then go into a second store selling the identical tape measure and pretend to steal a tape measure just like the one in your pocket. When arrested, let them go through the whole routine before showing proof of purchase. Sizeable out-of-court settlements may be had. Pick a store with a strict policy of prosecuting shoplifters. Also, be patient. It may take several weeks to get arrested. Some stores have very weak security. This can be done with a number of items where you put your name on the item in a hidden area. The item, however, should be something that a person would have reason to have while shopping. Small pocket calculators, folding knives, watches, cameras, small radios, and expensive pens are some items that come to mind.

Some retail stores require tailor-made acts to get cold revenge, such as a florist. Here is where chemicals or additives might come in handy. Calling and ordering flowers delivered to places and charged to someone else, perhaps another enemy, would put them in their place. How about going out to the cemetery and ordering a hundred wreaths for specific graves on Memorial Day. The graves could be those of veterans and the order could be billed to the local veteran's organization or one of the funeral homes in your area. Something like this combines a good deed with a measure of cold revenge added for dessert.

The thing to remember when dealing with retail stores is that every store has a weak underbelly somewhere. Find that weakness and you can do almost anything to them, sometimes even closing down the entire operation. When your enemy is a retail store, study the operation until you know it as well, if not better, than they do. Then you will be ready to safely exact your full measure of cold revenge.

14.
Apartments

High on the list of people most deserving a generous measure of cold revenge are apartment owners and managers. Likewise the ground lease in a mobile home park can lead to many of the same problems experienced in apartments. Generally speaking, the problems experienced with apartments, houses, or other dwelling arrangements derive from the desire of the owner or manager to have power over those who rent from him. The managers for some reason seem to have all the characteristics of petty gestapo agents. Their desire to harass other people is a philia. They seem unable to help themselves and thereby make life miserable for those who lease from them. Fortunately, the renter has at his disposal a full arsenal of means to exact a good measure of cold revenge.

Apartment managers are notorious for refusing to refund cleaning and damage deposits. These deposits are not, as we are led to believe, used to clean the unit for the next tenant. They go straight into the landlord's pocket. What can we do about it? Through our system of justice, nothing. Remember, those who hear these cases are just like the scum who cheated you out of the deposit. The only route left is cold revenge. To make the landlords earn the fee a hundred times over is the best course of action.

Damage preventing the manager from renting an apartment out again is one of the best tactics. If you can do enough damage to keep the unit off the market for several months, the jerk who cheated you will not forget you very soon. How about motor oil or ink on the carpet? If the apartment has common recreational facilities, such as a swimming pool, it is highly effective to damage these areas since the management will have all the tenants on its back to get them fixed. Again, your old friend motor oil in the pool will cause a major shutdown. This little act can be accomplished long after you've departed. The night before a long holiday weekend is by far the best time. Motor oil also works well in washers and dryers. A can of it on the pool table is a good calling card.

Sometimes it is better to do things that will have a time-bomb effect—it will go unnoticed but will explode later. Disconnect all the electrical receptacles and pull out as much wire as possible and cut it off so the receptacles cannot be rewired. The next tenant will surely want some compensation for the inconvenience. Wreck the air conditioning unit in the winter so that it won't show up until summer. Or cause the refrigerator or range to malfunction later, so that it will go unnoticed until used.

Since a person doesn't usually have a reason for cold revenge until he has moved out, damage to the inside of the apartment is usually out of the question. But if you strongly suspect your deposit will be withheld based on what has happened to other tenants, you can plan on having the manager really earn your deposit. There is no limit to what you can do to an apartment. Paint and soot on the wall surfaces and ceiling will keep the unit off the market for quite awhile. Plugging the toilets will cause even more distress to a penny-pinching manager. If you turn off the water and cut through the plumbing you will surely drive any manager around the bend when he turns the water back on and the plumbing system is a sieve. Then there is always superglue in the locks. What about putting it in his locks? Reread the chapter on superglue for additional ideas.

Mobile home park managers are one of the biggest targets of cold revenge. These parks are usually owned and managed by some of the lowest, most self-righteous scum on the planet. They pull every move in the book to make life miserable for the tenants. And they are well aware that it can cost thousands to move a mobile home and if you choose to sell, they make selling as difficult as possible. They demand a commission on the sale and if you move the unit, they will request an exit fee of several hundred dollars. Granted, most states have laws against such action, but look at who enforces the law. Motor oil in the pool, washers, and dryers is a good start. Cutting TV cable lines, plugging sewer lines, and generally disrupting park equipment and service usually makes life uncomfortable for the mobile park parasites. For those who live in mobile home parks, it is best that you study and plan your operation well in advance. Even if you have good management now, you will sooner or later end up with management that is just plain bad.

In the case of rental houses, there are additional things you can do to a house that is not practical in an apartment. One is cutting the floor joist almost through so the floor will sag and fail at a later date—sometimes as much as a year later. Another good one is the deliberate infusion of termites into a frame house in areas where termites are common. Properly done, these termites can truly be a time bomb bringing down a house in a couple of years. Leaky roofs seldom show up right away since the water must first soak through the insulation before the wallboard. This process can take months in a dry climate.

More specific things you might consider on a rented house are partially cutting through the water pipes, removing the insulation where the cuts are made, and hiding the loss of insulation by putting back the outer layer of the wrap. It may be years before the pipes freeze and break, but the wait will be worth it. Destroy the septic system by putting a large quantity of chlorine bleach into it. You can also put beetles into the carpets, kill the lawn, and almost cut through overhanging tree limbs to produce a perfect time-bomb effect.

There is no doubt that owners and managers of apartments, houses, and mobile home parks rate high on the list of people who deserve some cold revenge crammed down their throats. Let your imagination run wild and you will certainly discover many interesting things to do to these parasites of our society.

15.
Airlines

The airlines will sometimes deserve revenge because of the impersonal service they have lowered themselves to. Reservation clerks don't care enough to double-check your flight to see if, in fact, you can make your connection. Baggage handlers couldn't care less if your luggage goes in the opposite direction. Stewardesses are more interested in whom they are going to sleep with at their turn-around base than checking on the needs of the passengers. Pilots are obsessed with the coming strike and making more money and the mechanics couldn't care less whether the airplanes are properly maintained. So what if an engine falls off or the landing gear collapses. They just finished their strike with a fat pay raise and the safety checks aren't their responsibility anyway. It's up to the main base to take care of them. You begin to wonder what they really do for a living.

By far, the most common complaints about the airlines are lost baggage and being bumped off a flight because of over-booking. Few people complain about the crashes because there are few survivors. You must remember that no matter how angry you become with an airline, never blow your cool and threaten them. Don't even threaten to take them to court. Anyone who raises his voice in an airport terminal is automatically considered crazy and will be held for observation for several hours minimum. The number of crashes and hijackings has made everyone very nervous. If you raise your voice it doesn't matter what you say. There will be at least a dozen people who will swear you made violent threats. Under no conditions should you ever make a threat of violence—you may never see the light of day again.

This leaves very few options for cold revenge. You could make dozens of false reservations by phone, but this wouldn't bother the airlines—they will take as many reservations as come in. Should everyone show, they simply shuffle the surplus to other flights or other carriers. You will simply be wasting your time. This leaves the baggage system as the only weak underbelly that you can attack. Claiming your luggage to be lost is quite simple at most terminals. Simply collect your baggage, take it away, and check it into a locker. Then show your baggage claim tickets to the people in charge and demand that they locate it. After several weeks, they will give up and offer a settlement. Demand twice what they offer, but remember not to threaten. Simply tell them that you feel it would be better if your lawyer handled the claim. The last thing an airline wants is to get involved in litigation over baggage.

Granted, this isn't much of an act of revenge, but it's about as good as you'll get in these days of terrorism and hijacking. At least take heart in the fact that the airlines themselves have a tendency to destroy each other in their quest for a larger share of the market. Almost every major airline has been on the ropes in the recent past, and it is likely they will all be back there again in the near future. Airlines are much like the utility companies in the way they are run and in the way they are governed by federal agencies. The people who run the airlines are really civil servants. The public will just have to get used to that fact and hope they will not have the need for cold revenge with the airlines.

Airlines, however, can be a useful tool in getting cold revenge against an enemy. Cancel his reservation during the heavy travel season, and he will very likely be unable to get a flight. If you are in a position to be with your enemy when he checks in, switch his luggage labels making them go astray. Another thing you can do is to slip a few rounds of ammunition or a wicked looking knife into his coat pocket before he goes through the metal detector. This is always good for a laugh and will cause him a great deal of embarrassment.

For those who are bolder, lead the airline to believe they

are going to be hijacked. This can be accomplished with a single phone call. The airlines do not take calls of this nature lightly, in fact, they have a tendency to overreact. These scares will cause delays and lots of trouble. In turn, it could lead to an investigation, which means trouble for you. Risk this only if your desire for cold revenge is really strong. Otherwise, stick with the baggage routine.

16.
Magazine Subscriptions

Magazine subscriptions may seem an unusual tool for cold revenge, but can be very powerful. The technique is equally applicable to book clubs, record and tape clubs, collectors clubs, such as spoons, thimbles, ceramics, medals, and an endless variety of other collectables advertised in the Sunday newspaper magazine supplement. It also includes any other item procured as a club member on a monthly basis, such as fruit of the month clubs where members receive a selection of seasonal fruits each month. And to a lesser degree, these techniques apply to the everyday garden variety of mail-order houses. It would be wise to study up on mail-order laws when planning any operation of this nature.

The use of magazine subscriptions to obtain revenge will largely depend on the type of enemy you have. If he is a calm, collected individual where small things do not bother him, it is doubtful that these methods will have much effect on him. However, if he is high-strung, as most petty parasites are, you will find it easy to get your revenge with little or no risk.

Gather up every order form from every magazine in your local library. You will have well over a hundred magazine subscription application forms on postcards with no postage necessary. You will also find a host of order forms for bookclubs, record clubs, etc. Fill these out with your enemy's name and address, check the box to be billed later, and mail them in. Mail them in small groups from several post offices so as not to draw attention to your act. Then, collect catalogs from various mail-order houses and order in your enemy's name. Have it all shipped C.O.D., if possible. If this is done enthusiastically ongoingly, your enemy should receive sacks of mail. Then the bills will come. Consider the effect if you did it again using your enemy's address of employment. When you gather these magazine subscription forms, you will probably have two or more copies of each. Why not have your enemy swamped at both his home and office. To save yourself the trouble of filling out these applications, have a rubber stamp made with your enemy's name and address. Have it made out of town and pay cash.

This tactic does not end with filling your enemy's mailbox with mountains of unwanted mail. You can also have copies of porno magazines sent to his place of employment or his home. Another idea, if your enemy is a banker, would be to send a paramilitary magazine to his office. Then there are the current gay magazines, the mere possession of which would start tongues wagging. Add to this some embarrassing merchandise delivered to your enemy's office. Even if he doesn't open it there, the fact that it came in a plain brown wrapper will be sufficient to blow his mind.

These tactics of cold revenge fall into two distinct categories. The first, as has been discussed above, consists of subscriptions and mail-orders being used as tools. In the second category these entities become the object of your strategies. What do you do when a magazine or mail-order club gets on your back for not paying for material sent to you, or better still, *not* sent to you?

Consider the case where the magazines, or whatever, get on your back for not paying for a subscription. So what— hardly a reason for putting into effect big plans for cold revenge. Simply ignore them. They can't do anything except send statements and have some phony collection agency make a little noise. You can be assured that you will never be attacked or taken prisoner by a collection agency which sends a bulk-rate letter. If these letters annoy you, the law states that you can advise the agency to take action. They must then stop sending the collection letters and proceed with court or other action. This is seldom done and you can claim you never received any of what they say they sent you. The burden of proof is on them.

The best thing to do when harassed by one of these parasites is to simply ignore them. If you are still annoyed, collect a bunch of order forms for the magazine or entity in question and send them in with phony names and addresses.

17.
Property Liens

One of the best forms of cold revenge is to have liens placed against your enemy's property. Doing this is easier than one may think. A lien on real property is a claim. A mortgage or deed of trust is a lien on real property. Other liens can include mechanic's or materialman's liens which are filed with the court for work and materials used in building, remodeling, or repairing real property. Examples are a new roof, added room, or repair of fire damage. Another way for a lien to be placed against a piece of property is having a judgment placed against the owner, which can be for almost anything. An auto accident can result in a very high judgment. Other judgments that can result in liens come from petty crimes such as one handled in small claims court. Remember the example of the auto repair mechanic who was in bed with the judge? These things can result in liens against real property. The object is then to decide how this system of placing liens can be best used against your enemy.

Procuring a lien normally requires going to court with a claim, getting a judgment, and having it entered in the court records in the county where your enemy has property. Unless you have a legitimate claim, it's a dead end. Even if you have a legitimate claim, chances are the court will not be in your favor as there is a good chance the judge and your enemy are friends. If your enemy is in business in a small town, it is likely that he and the judge belong to the same clubs and socialize. There is always that unwritten agreement where the judge agrees to protect his friend so long as he is taken care of. It follows then that using the courts would not be a very prudent move. Actually, the furthest you can stay away from the courts, the better, and certainly the more effective you will be in exacting revenge.

How then do you get a lien against your enemy? Simple, you fake it. That is to say, you make up phony judgments and record them with the county. Most county clerks are so bored with their jobs they don't take a second look at what comes in to record. Even if they did, they are too incompetent to know what it is. For the most part, they are too busy talking about their last date and being concerned about their next. It would be a good idea to learn everything there is to know about the recorder's office personnel and procedures, how the recordings are made and what becomes of the paper. Learn about the fees involved and always pay them in cash. Do not draw attention to yourself. If by some rare chance you find a clerk who knows what he is doing, avoid him when you make your recording. Learn when he goes to lunch, or better still is on vacation, and take your judgment in at that time.

Once a judgment against your enemy is recorded, it becomes a lien on all his real property. But nothing actually happens at this point. To collect the judgment, you must bring about a foreclosing suit to force payment or sale of the property to satisfy the judgment. Naturally, you won't do this because the judgment is fake and it is in favor of some person, perhaps another enemy, or some mythical person or organization. Now the lien becomes a time bomb. Nothing will happen until your enemy sells his house or other real property, tries to borrow against its equity, or applies for a sizeable loan, where the lender checks the court record to see if there are any outstanding judgments. This might be years in the future. It is best that the judgment be in favor of a mythical person, because they will have to track him down before the judgment is vacated. This alone can take a year or more and will certainly compound the interest on your cold revenge. If you put the judgment in the name of another one of your enemies, he will have a lot of explaining to do when that well-known product hits the fan. If you are planning to leave town, be sure to record the liens in a name similar to your own so that your enemy will know for sure where his problem came from.

All the above may sound like a lot of fun and may also appear very risky and complicated. Actually, it is very easy to bring about, so easy that you can leave a trail behind you if you're not careful. You should get a fake notary seal—one of the easiest things to accomplish in the operation. Get it in another name and use a mail drop. You can get applications to become a notary at almost any stationery store or write the secretary of state for an application form. Doing this will not make the notary commission official, but that's not important. All you need is an official-looking seal to get documents recorded. While you're waiting for your notary commission to be approved, attend a few court sessions and get the feel for how they do things. Confine your visits to civil cases and proceedings instead of criminal cases. Try to hit the court on a day where they are cleaning up lots of odds and ends. Find the most senile judge you can, which won't be too difficult since half of the judges are senile and the other half are corrupt.

Now you must prepare a summons and complaint against your enemy. Do this by going to the court records and copying a case for a claim already in the file. This may take a little research, but when you find the right case it will simply be a matter of changing the names. Then, fill out an affidavit of service and notarize it with your fake notary seal. Remember the service must not actually take place as the one who supposedly performed the service is also a mythical person. In fact, everyone except your enemy and the judge are mythical. Your package now consists of a summons and complaint and an affidavit of service. These you have copied from an existing case in the court files, changing the names to match your enemy's and other mythical people. Issue these documents to the recorder and wait for a court date to be assigned. Do not appear in court on the assigned day, in fact, don't go anywhere near the court that day. If no one appears, the court sets the case aside assuming a settlement was made.

Next, prepare a motion for default and an order for default. Since your enemy did not actually get served, you are claiming a judgment by default. However, you don't actually want to appear before a judge for this purpose. To do this correctly, go to the courtroom of the senile judge you have chosen on a day when a lot of things are happening in court. You have already obtained a copy of the judge's signature and have duplicated it until it looks like his. In fact, you have already signed his name to the order of default. When you are satisfied that this is a day when such a case as yours could have come before this senile judge, add the date and drop it in the recorder's "in" basket. The wheels of justice will slowly get it into the computer, and your enemy will have judgment and an automatic lien on his property that may not become known to him for years. The longer it takes for your deed to come to light, the more difficult it will be to straighten it out. If the judge whose signature you forged has passed on to that great warped bench in the sky, it will be next to impossible for them to prove it was not his signature. Your enemy may have to spend hundreds or even thousands of dollars to clear the title on his property—something the court is reluctant to do, in view of the fact that the judgment holder may someday surface and prove his claim.

It is a lot of work to get a judgment in the records, but once accomplished it will be one of your finest moments that few have the courage to create and bring about. Don't leave a trail, and study your local court procedures to be sure the work looks authentic. This is one of the best time-bomb acts in the book and is well worth the time and energy it takes to pull it off.

18.
Drugs and Additives

Drugs and cold revenge are a conundrum each person must work out for themselves. For the purpose of this book, drugs are classified into two groups; recreational drugs such as marijuana, cocaine, LSD, angel dust (PCP), and other forms of illegal drugs; and prescription and over-the-counter drugs. Both of these types of drugs are used in cold revenge.

The use of prescription and over-the-counter drugs has been advocated by many writers as a means of pulling a practical joke. These acts are absurdly stupid. A laxative in the chocolate chip cookies may sound like a lot of fun and games, but the person who has a physical problem and goes overboard on the cookies might have such a violent reaction that serious hospitalization or death may result. More often than not, this is usually an innocent bystander. Even the use of an additive to cause someone's urine to change color can be dangerous. The reaction to these additives cannot always be predicted and tragic results may occur. They are not for the connoisseur of cold revenge. The person who is seeking cold revenge should stick with methods that will yield the best effect on his enemy. Practical jokes, which the above schemes are aimed at, are not a tool of cold revenge because the results are not predictable and are not usually aimed at your enemy specifically. It is strongly suggested that this line of action be left to the college fraternity boys in their childish gatherings.

Recreational drugs are also avoided by the true extractor of cold revenge. We do not judge the morality of these drugs, but since they are illegal, using them for cold revenge can open a can of worms that leads to far more trouble than the project is worth. There is some justification for using these drugs for purposes of entrapment, but it is recommended to trap only a drug pusher. Procuring enough drugs to make a good case of entrapment against your enemy will not only cost a lot of money, but will surely draw attention to the drug dealers. Unless you are prepared to take on this consequence, it is not worth the effort.

Some of the other additives and chemicals do have their place in the art of cold revenge. Sugar in the gas tank has been a very popular one over the years. Butyric acid is another useful chemical, which is good for really stinking up an office or public building. The use of additives can be very dangerous if the user doesn't know what he is doing. Make sure you know the end result. In using additives, there are a limited number of things you can accomplish. The prime accomplishments are to cause corrosion, contamination, abrasion, or adulteration. These accomplishments are usually not as important as the chain reaction they cause. For example, sugar in the gas tank stops the engine, but primarily causes your enemy the trouble of getting it repaired. Also, when he finds out what happened, he will really blow his cool and that is what cold revenge is all about.

Sulfuric acid is another excellent product that causes corrosion—it will corrode almost any metal and it is readily available from auto batteries. Oil, of course, will contaminate water such as in a swimming pool. Contaminating an auto battery with baking soda will kill it in a few minutes. Emery dust will serve as an excellent abrasive, and so will good old sand. Try these in your enemy's crankcase oil. A classic example of adulteration would be salt in the sugar. Salt is also an excellent corrosive. For more information on chemical reactions, a primer on chemistry is helpful. Always remember that when dealing with chemicals, such as acids, there are risks involved such as explosions or other undesirable reactions. If you don't know what you are doing with strange chemicals, leave them alone. You are better off spending your time and money in areas within your expertise.

19.
Contractors

Contractors of all kinds are prime candidates for deserving cold revenge. Few do what they promise or contract to do and cost overruns are common—not just small overruns, but many exceed 50 percent. These contractors have been ripping off the public for decades and usually have close ties with the judicial system in the area where they operate. When you see a contractor fined or even jailed, it does not mean the system is working; it means that a contractor has not made proper arrangements with the judicial system to split the profits, or refused to do some free work on a judge's or prosecutor's home. This is an age-old problem. Honest contractors try to set up a business and they are quickly in deep trouble. The Planning Department won't issue permits, and then the building inspector won't approve the work. These contractors would be surprised what putting on an inexpensive roof for the judge would do to their greasing the wheels of the permits and inspection process.

There are two categories of contractors: those who deal in public works contracts, such as roads and public buildings; and those who build for the individual, such as homes and remodeling work. Those who deal in public works certainly rip the public off to a far greater extent than the contractor for the individual. As a private citizen, you most likely will want cold revenge against the individual contractor. This can become difficult as most of these parasites enjoy the protection of the court, or are fly-by-night operations. But there is one good way to get cold revenge on them. That is with the tract-home builder. The contractors who build tract homes usually deserve revenge. They cheat at every stage of construction. If there is a corner to cut, they cut it, then cut it again. Is it any wonder that the quality of homes has dropped so low? If you have bought a new tract home from a contractor, you most likely had problems getting him to make repairs. This is very typical of home building contractors, but there is a way to even the score with these parasites.

The easiest way is to sabotage their work. This is best done during construction. One of the easiest and most effective ways is cutting the electrical wiring at each receptacle. This should be done after the insulation is in and just prior to the installation of the wallboard, which limits the sabotage to the exterior walls of the house. With the insulation in place, it is next to impossible to see these cut wires, and when the wallboard is in place, the sabotage will not be detected until the owner moves in and tries to use the facilities. In one case, a builder had to tear out the wallboard in most of the house to make the repairs. It was very costly, and so was the addition of the night watchman to prevent a recurrence of such acts. The joke was that this sabotage was committed during the day while workmen were about. It is easy to gain access to houses while under construction. You can say you are the prospective owner, or are planning to have that builder do one for you. If it is a tract, say you are considering buying one and want to see the quality of construction. Still another fool-proof way into the houses is to get some real estate business cards with any name on them, and say you are pre-viewing the home. The workmen couldn't care less.

Once inside the house, there are unlimited things you can do, depending on the stage of construction. Don't try to do too much at the early stages. They are likely to be discovered. Areas of sabotage that are most effective are, as described, the electrical system. And if you have the time alone, crosswire the circuits in such a way that it becomes impossible to keep a circuit breaker closed. It may also create a lot of smoke. In any event, the builder will lose many customers since things like this quickly spread through the buying public's grapevine.

The plumbing system can be screwed up in several ways. Switch the hot and cold waterlines at the sinks. Today, these are usually made of flexible metal connecting lines or plastic tubing, both of which are easy to switch. For the more adventurous, take a section of the drain line apart and stuff it with something to make a permanent plug. A tennis ball works very well on the smaller lines, and a small beach ball works on the larger lines. Heating units and kitchen appliances are easy things to disrupt. A couple of switched wires will actually cause more chaos than cut wires. Study the construction of these appliances and other ways to sabotage them will come to light.

Should you be an unhappy buyer, you can also picket the sales office, which will put doubt into the minds of many prospective buyers. However, this is a legitimate means of protest, something that most seekers of cold revenge will not do.

Although these methods of sabotage are aimed primarily at the contractor, they can be used in another way. That is, if your enemy is building a new house, you can keep track of the building progress and sabotage along the way. Building a new house is traumatic enough, but when you add these little extra problems, your enemy will really be a basket case.

20.
The Post Office

Post offices are much like telephone companies—they manifest as a double-edged sword. They are actually more useful in extracting cold revenge than they are deserving in getting it. There is little a post office can do to cause you to want revenge against it. However, there are some employees that take it upon themselves to decide which mail will be returned and which they will make an effort to deliver. An example of this kind of jerk is illustrated in the following example. A letter was addressed to the city library of a small town in Colorado. This town has a population of about eight-thousand people. The address was something like 17 N. Main Street. Because of a typographical error, the letter was addressed to 71 N. Main Street. Now both 17 and 71 are odd numbers and would be on the same side of the street, and in fact, the first block of N. Main Street. Still, the letter was returned rubberstamped in red ink as incorrectly addressed. Now how many city libraries can there be in the first block of N. Main Street in a small town in Colorado? How many city libraries in the whole town? This was obviously the act of a petty individual, which can lead to revenge letting him know that he is there to serve the public and not to harass others with his petty self-important actions.

Remember that post offices are under the protection of the federal government. They, like the banks, enjoy a protective blanket, which tends to lead them into the realm of not giving a damn about the public who they are supposed to serve.

There are a few ways to get back at the post office. One

is your old friend, superglue. Glue the locks on a dozen or so boxes frequently and drive the postmaster crazy. Glue the pens to the desk in the lobby and make them look like a bunch of jerks. Another way is to jam the systems with dead letters. This is done by sending letters containing blank paper to nonexistent addresses with no return address. Expensive? Not at all—a one-cent stamp will carry a letter to its destination and the receiver will then have to pay the postage due. If it cannot be delivered at the destination and there is no return address, it goes to the dead letter office. You can also jam the system without even using a stamp, or perhaps by putting on used stamps. In any event, you can cause a lot of extra work and give them some reason to wonder why anyone would want to hurt the post office.

The other way to view the post office, like the telephone company, is that it can provide a tool for getting the cold revenge you justly deserve. Through the post office you can gather information about your enemy and spread false information about him. The mail, however, is a little more dangerous than the phone in spreading and gathering information. Written evidence is left behind. Care must be taken as to what kind of information you spread and gather.

A more subtle use of the mail for cold revenge is to flood your enemy with magazines and junk mail. This and other use of the printed word were discussed previously. The mail can be used to embarrass and intimidate your enemy in such a way that he will self-destruct. This is the best way to use the mail. Never make threats in writing through the mail, including an innuendo of a threat. The courts will treat it as a threat. Embarrassment can be easily obtained by simply sending mail to your enemy's place of work with an embarrassing return address—focus on your enemy's particular hang-ups. A letter with a state or federal penitentiary and name of someone with his last name as a return address will send some people around the bend. A heavily perfumed letter will do the same to others. These things are what you need to find out during your planning and information gathering. The importance of knowing these things will save you a lot of trial and error and wasted time. Learn your enemy better than he knows himself, and you will be able to make the most effective use of the mail to get your cold revenge.

One thing to bear in mind is that the postal system is part of the government, and as such the workers within it try to impress their supervisors. They feel that by blowing the whistle on someone, they are making points. Therefore, do not do a great deal through your own post office. Work through other post offices, or better still, through a mail drop.

21.
Curses

Curses to get cold revenge? Why not? Anything that will cause your enemy distress is a good tool for cold revenge. A curse, as you know, is an appeal or prayer for evil or injury to befall someone or something. Most of us do not believe in the power of a curse until we witness something that proves it can work. A curse was once put on a courthouse and the employees took up a collection to have an Indian medicine man take it off. This was on the West Coast in the eighties. They all joked about it, but deep down most of these people had an uneasy feeling about the curse. How effective a curse can be on your enemy depends on his feelings about curses. This is something you should endeavor to find out during the planning and information gathering stages of your program.

Should you find that your enemy has a tendency to believe and fear supernatural phenomena, then you are in an excellent position to cause him to self-destruct. Send him a voodoo doll of his likeness and your work is over.

Do not use the mails to send the doll as this could be construed as a threat or at least a form of harassment. Send it by messenger.

Another form of curse involves giving the enemy an object or trinket that supposedly carries the curse or spell. The enemy is then informed of the curse and brings it about through his own psyche. This is the general outlook of the average Westerner. Whether or not this is actually true is not the scope of this book. Making your enemy believe he is cursed can be just as good as the real thing. Let's say you have worked out a curse and have your enemy sweating on it, then you add to its authenticity by doing something like slashing all the tires on his car. Your enemy will think it is part of the curse if you leave another trinket like the original at the scene. This type of action can be ongoing for as long as you wish, and can have far-reaching effects and rewards.

The trinkets that are used in this way look authentic if they are crudely made and look like they were carved with primitive tools. Foreign coins from countries where these arts are practiced work well with a rough hole cut through the center and pieces of beaded raw-hide or string running through the middle. Other objects, such as pieces of wood, metal, ceramic, bone, and glass; or even bottle caps, checkers, or dominoes can be used. Be sure you can duplicate them, but don't keep a stack of them laying around where they can be found and used as evidence against you.

The delivery of the trinket to your enemy will present some problem, as you do not want to be exposed to him as the source this early in the game. Leave it on his desk or at his office, or send it to him with a message. One person used the old "Treasure Island" black spot effectively in 1981. It is a simple but very effective technique when used against an enemy who believes in black magic or even with one who doesn't know what he believes in, which is the case with most of the bullies and scum of the world.

More people should use these psychological tools against their enemies. They are among the best in getting cold revenge because they match one for one the system the parasites use to intimidate those they hold power over. Petty servants will always fear the supernatural. The next time you have a hassle, give him a trinket and tell him that a great misfortune will happen. Then go out and smash his windshield. Before long, word will get around and your life will be made a lot easier. You may not be able to eliminate these parasites from our society, but you may force some of them into early retirement.

22.
Potpourri

There are many things one can use and many things one can do to get a measure of cold revenge and there is no way to catalog all of them in a single volume such as this. Many other people and institutions worthy of revenge could have been covered in this book, but the acts of revenge could have been similar to what we have already discussed.

However, there are some institutions that warrant mention here, as well as a few acts that can be taken against them. Among them are automobile dealers. There are many reasons why you may want measure of cold revenge against them. They do everything from not honoring the warranty on a car to giving bad service. Motor oil or ink on the seats of a new car will make their day. Plan this for a weekend when there is a sale and do it to the best model on the showroom floor. Your utility knife will come in handy to slice the seats and door panels. You can also do a lot of damage under the hood with a little know-how. Damage the tires or take the car for a test drive and leave it on some side street. On this one you'll have to walk into the dealership while they are busy and they won't notice you did not have a car on the lot when you arrived.

If your enemy happens to be a real bastard and has children, try turning him in for child abuse. Just play the part of a concerned neighbor or relative—you won't have to even give a name and chances are anyway that he does abuse his children. It's the nature of these parasites who deserve a mouthful of cold revenge. In today's society, child abuse is greatly frowned on. The government has great bureaucracies set up to handle these cases. These bureaus are staffed with many highly educated parasites, who can find work only in these gestapo oriented quasi-police agencies. In order to get ahead, each case worker must bring as many cases as possible for prosecution. You can be sure that any report of child abuse will have a host of case workers on it who intend to make names for themselves. These case workers have such a killer instinct that they will usually make a case even if there isn't any evidence. You have another thing on your side when pulling this act: the children themselves will usually help hang their parents these days. This is probably one of the best acts you can do, as the news will always get back to your enemy's employer as the case workers will investigate every aspect of his life. Even if the charge is unfounded, all the people who the case workers contacted will believe he is guilty.

Charity can be used as a tool against your enemy. Simply give his name to all the local charities as a pledge or volunteer. Call the next charity telethon and make a sizable donation using his name. Make your call from a phone booth and hang around for awhile. They sometimes check by calling back to confirm large donations.

There are times you may want information about your enemy and you need to make face-to-face contact with the source of the information, such as his neighbors or employer. There is no better disguise than the clerical garb. People seldom remember anything beyond the fact that a minister or priest called on them. They will usually tell everything they know to a person dressed this way.

Computers can be tools for cold revenge. The most obvious use for the computer is to store information about your enemy and his activities. With a little programming, you should be able to use the computer to plan your operation. The computer can tell you the best time to execute your actions and keep track of your overall effectiveness. It can also write letters with an entirely different syntax than your own, thereby disguising you as the author. The computer can be used for mass mailing of literature. Your computer can do many things better and more quickly than you would ever imagine. Since home computers are currently being integrated into our society, there is still a lot to learn about using them for cold revenge. From what we read and hear about teenagers being able to get into the various government computers, it is evident that one could use these techniques to promote cold revenge. Let's say you could alter your enemy's bank records. That would cause him a lot of problems, and if he knew it could be done over and over again, he would soon be in quite a state. Even more diabolical would be to extensively alter his government data, such as his social security records. This time bomb might not be discovered for years.

It is apparent that if you are a computer literate you have a powerful tool to use against your enemy. However, what if a computer is giving *you* problems or you wish to disable your enemy's computer. That is easy to fix. One of the easiest and most effective methods is to tape a powerful magnet to the bottom of his floppy disk file box. It may take months before he figures out why he loses so much data and has so many errors on his computer. This is a good act to do just before leaving the employ of a company that has dumped repeatedly on you over the years.

There are some jerks who are terminal lechers, or dirty old men. Whether your reason for cold revenge is associated with this trait is immaterial, but it can be used as a means of getting all the cold revenge you will ever need. The use of a hooker with herpes or a venereal disease will serve the purpose very well. There are some problems associated with this operation. First, it may be well beyond the average person's expertise to bring all the pieces together. Second, you must involve other people and you may be creating a real epidemic. But if you can pull this one off and give your enemy a lifetime gift of herpes, you will truly have gotten revenge. Once you have put the hooker and your enemy together, spread the word that your enemy has VD so others will be warned. There is no point in innocent people getting involved.

Graffiti is another tool of cold revenge. Use your enemy's name in association with something you know will cause him distress. If you found out that your enemy is against the use of arms, then your graffiti should associate him with the NRA or another pro-gun organization. If he is anti-abortion, then

link him to pro-choice. The application of graffiti to cold
revenge is strictly psychological in nature and any real damage
done will be by your enemy's own self-destructive mind.

There may come the day when you are faced with loosing
your home for some reason that is no fault of your own. When
this happens, you must first get your feet back on the ground,
so to speak, and when you get over the shock, you can begin
to put into effect a plan of cold revenge against whomever
caused you this grief. The best philosophy here is to leave
nothing behind to the enemy, but don't burn the place down.
This will be considered a criminal act and you could serve
several years in prison. The prime reason for this is that the
courts and the lending institutions work together to cheat the
public out of their property. Chances are loosing your home
will be coupled with the loss of a job. It then follows that you
may leave the area to search for another job. If this is the case,
you will have little fear and you can do all the things described
in the chapter on apartments and even go further. You could
undermine the foundations so the house will sag and maybe
even collapse. Another thing you can do to the lending institution is to take a chainsaw and cut every stud in the house almost
through. Make sure the electrical power is off when you do
this and be careful not to cause a premature collapse by cutting
too many. Also, don't leave a window unbroken and certainly
do not leave an appliance or drape behind. Actually, what you
are trying to do is leave them a situation where it will be
considered too costly to tear down—a nice gift of cold revenge.

Finale

The joy of cold revenge is within the reach of anyone who wants to make things a little more even in our society. It is time the greedy scum and parasites learned that they can't get away with dumping on people and have the courts back them up. When the courts learn that the people want their freedom and liberty as promised in the Constitution back in the hands of the people, the more likely this nation will avert a class revolution. You as a person who has sought cold revenge have placed yourself in the position of being a pioneer.

It is the responsibility of every individual to resist tyranny in any form. Doing anything less is to risk losing the foundation of this society. Doing anything less is an invitation for those with gestapo mentalities to continue to grind the rights of the people into the mud. Thomas Jefferson said it best, "Resistance to tyrants is obedience to God."